THE PRIMAL BLUEPRINT COOKBOOK

MARK SISSON
with **JENNIFER MEIER**

The Primal Blueprint Cookbook

Library of Congress Control Number: 2010924523

Library of Congress Cataloging-in-Publication Data
Sisson, Mark, 1953–

The Primal Blueprint Cookbook / Mark Sisson with Jennifer Meier

ISBN 978-0-9822077-2-7
1. Cooking 2. Health 3. Diet 4. Low Carb

Editor/Project Manager: Aaron Fox
Design/Layout: Kristin Roybal
Consultants: Anna Salvesen, Jennifer Zotalis, Bradford Hodgson, Reagan Smith

For more information about the *Primal Blueprint*, please visit www.primalblueprint.com
For information on quantity discounts, please call 888-774-6259

Publisher: Primal Nutrition, Inc.
23805 Stuart Ranch Rd. Suite 145
Malibu, CA 90265

ACKNOWLEDGMENTS

First of all, this book couldn't have assumed its present form without valuable input from tens of thousands of regular readers at my blog, MarksDailyApple.com. The insights and direction from this vibrant community guide my Primal explorations on a daily basis.

My co-author Jennifer Meier worked tirelessly to not only bring rich flavor and life to these menu ideas, but she took every single photograph in the book. Maybe her kitchen will stay clean for at least a few days in a row now! Aaron Fox, my general manager and MarksDailyApple.com webmaster, was instrumental in coordinating the efforts of everyone involved in this project, and in editing the Primal Blueprint Cookbook. MarksDailyApple.com staffers Jennifer Zotalis, Bradford Hodgson and Reagan Smith offered excellent insights to help improve the text and provided research and fact-checking support. Gratitude to Anna Salvesen for her early guidance in preparing several of these recipes. My ace designer Kristin Roybal was single-handedly responsible for the fabulous design and layout of both the text and the cover.

Special thanks to my wife Carrie and children Devyn and Kyle for allowing me the space to sometimes push the limits of accepted culinary wisdom.

TABLE OF CONTENTS

INTRODUCTION

Primal. Paleo. Low-carb. Gluten-free. Dairy-free. These are all at least partially descriptive of the latest revolution in cuisine—a revolution that eschews grains, man made fats and other processed foods in favor of tastier, more natural fare. It's also a revolution that promises to let you enjoy sumptuous feasts of some of nature's most satisfying foods, while allowing you to almost effortlessly lose excess body fat, improve energy levels, get sick less often and possibly even live longer.

Long ago, our hunter-gatherer ancestors feasted off the land—and sea. Foraging, fishing and hunting for their meals, they evolved to thrive on whatever they could pick, catch or spear. As a result, theirs was a rich and varied diet of plentiful meat, seafood, fowl, fresh vegetables and fruits, and wild nuts and seeds. With this natural bounty came a veritable trove of nutrients: copious antioxidants, polyphenols and minerals, ample protein, nourishing and sustaining fats. These are the nutrients our genes expect from us at every meal, the nutrients that ensure that we will be lean, fit, and healthy.

Fast forward to 10,000 years ago, and human health in much of the world took a decisive turn. The advent of the agricultural revolution overturned some 150,000+ years of hunter-gatherer sustenance. Grains, the centerpiece of cultivation, now largely supplanted the nutrient-rich foraging diet. As archeological evidence reveals, human health and stature took a blow with this nutritional downgrade. Despite this shift, the evolutionary hunter-gatherer blueprint continued to be passed down through each generation and, in fact, governs our bodies to this day.

More than ever now, we live in an aberrant culinary universe. Our culture's penchant for sugars, grains (including whole grains) and processed foods constitutes a striking—and costly—incongruity between what our bodies evolved to thrive on and what we actually feed them. We see the results in the surging lifestyle diseases that plague us today: obesity, heart disease, diabetes, arthritis, autoimmune disorders and more.

The answer, of course, lies in re-harmonizing our diets with our abiding evolutionary genetic mandate. This is exactly the heart of the Primal Blueprint, a constellation of lifestyle principles that seek to realign our daily life with our inherent physiological design. Informed by the elegant logic of biology, the Primal Blueprint model adapts the nutritional cornerstones of hunter-gatherer fare for the culinary tastes and unprecedented variety of the 21st century. I think you'll find that the recipes in this book represent the gratifying pinnacle of that convergence.

In this collection, you'll enjoy user-friendly recipes for Primal cuisine with incomparable flavor and sumptuousness as well as tips for creating your own Primal kitchen. These recipes are part of my own permanent rotation, and they never disappoint. Many of the selections in this book offer Primal versions of classic, comfortingly familiar dishes. Think succulent Italian pot roast with balsamic vinegar and herbs or rich chocolate custard. Other selections infuse popular ingredients with fresh, original tastes like tender shrimp cakes with coconut almond dressing or fried eggs over zesty green chili burgers.

Readers new to Primal eating might notice—but certainly won't miss—what these recipes don't include—specifically the grains that bulk up so many modern dishes. Despite the current love affair with whole grains, the fact remains that they provide few nutrients and introduce substances like gluten, lectins and phytates that disrupt our physiology rather than support it. Their minimal amount of protein, micronutrients and fiber are more efficiently obtained through more nourishing sources like antioxidant-rich vegetables and fruits and hearty meats. After all, it really isn't the grains themselves we relish in dishes but the savory sauces and meats, the flavorful herbs and veggies and other "toppings" that we add to them!

You'll also find that another staple of the modern diet, dairy, plays a limited and optional role in Primal recipes as it did for our hunter-gatherer ancestors. Although some dairy foods like pastured butter and aged cheeses can offer outstanding flavor and richness to Primal dishes, the preponderance of dairy in our modern diet again often displaces foods to which our genes are perhaps better adapted. The occasional and intentional use of dairy ingredients like pastured butter and cream in these recipes highlights their best nutrition and taste; however, non-dairy substitutions offer flavorful alternatives for those who don't wish to include dairy.

What you *will* find and truly savor in Primal fare, however, will reward both your senses and well-being. Welcome to a whole new eating experience: it's all about fulfillment—and vitality—from here on out!

Variety

Variety equals optimum nutrition—and taste. The typical modern diet revolves around a depressingly narrow selection of foods more limited than even our parents and grandparents enjoyed. The restriction not only diminishes the nutritional value of our meals, it's frankly unsatisfying. Primal cuisine restores our ancestors' culinary abundance and then some by taking full advantage of a wide-ranging 21st century assortment of meats, vegetables, fruits, nuts, seeds and herbs. With the likes of rosemary and bay-infused roasted lamb, tangy herb and caper marinade, and blackberry ginger mocktails, dinner will never be the same old, same old again.

Freshness

The fresher our food, the more nutritious it is. Freshness was obviously a key benefit to the traditional hunter-gatherer diet. In keeping, Primal eating maximizes nutrition and taste by favoring the freshest, most naturally grown/raised ingredients. Wherever possible, recipes prioritize pastured, organic seasonal and locally grown/raised ingredients. Imagine cream of greens soup made fresh after a farmers' market run. Or how about peachy chicken salad on a warm summer evening?

Richness

Among the highlights of Primal fare is the enjoyment of sumptuous, nourishing fats. For those uninitiated in the Primal Blueprint, Primal cooking makes liberal and gratifying use of healthy oils and "clean" animal fats (fats as free as possible from agricultural contaminants like growth hormones, antibiotics and pesticides). Although frequently and falsely maligned, certain select fats offer key nutrients unavailable in other foods—nutrients critical to the functioning of many physiological systems. Besides all that, many natural fats lend incredible flavor and more satisfaction to each dish. Envision a chopped yellowfin tuna salad rich with creamy avocado and thick bacon, or braised beef shanks with meat so tender it's falling off the bone. You'll wonder why you ever ate any other way.

Just as the Mark's Daily Apple blog and my recent book, *The Primal Blueprint*, share the essential principles behind the Primal Blueprint diet, this cookbook serves up some of the best that Primal eating has to offer. The recipes are ideal for Primal Blueprint adherents as well as those following Paleo, Atkins, South Beach, Zone and other low carb diets. Although the recipes are based on the Primal Blueprint, they're great for anyone looking to live a healthier life. If you want more from your eating experience—more flavor, more nutrients, more satisfaction, more vitality throughout your day, this book is for you! Whether or not you're currently a Primal Blueprint follower, I'm confident that you'll savor these dishes as outstanding samples of Primal eating—and enticing evidence that the Primal Blueprint is truly a recipe for thriving. Enjoy!

Sourcing Primal Ingredients

Before you turn on the stove or light the grill, the first step in making a recipe is gathering your ingredients. Keeping your kitchen well-stocked with a wide variety of fresh, healthy ingredients takes effort, there's no question about that. But shopping for food doesn't have to be a chore. It can even be fun once you start discovering new ingredients and new ways to source them.

Use all your senses when you shop—touch and smell produce, let yourself be drawn towards bright, fresh colors and be curious. Read labels, ask questions and try things you've never tried before. Begin establishing relationships with the people you buy food from—you'll be surprised how much you'll learn.

No matter where you live, you probably have more options than you think when it comes to gathering ingredients. If you can't find a specific ingredient for a recipe though, don't sweat it. Use whatever you have on hand or even better, what's fresh and in season.

Grocery Stores

For most of us, whether it's because of economics or convenience, shopping at supermarkets is an inevitable part of life. Luckily, you'll be able to find many Primal foods in supermarkets. Supermarkets are a great place to stock up on frozen and canned foods or items you might want to buy in larger quantities. Specialty markets, co-ops, ethnic markets and online retailers often carry the harder-to-find ingredients that regular supermarkets don't. Wherever you shop, just make sure to read the labels so you know exactly what's in the food you're buying.

Farmers' Markets and Roadside Produce Stands

Go directly to the source. These days, most cities hold farmers' markets at various times during the week where you can buy most of your produce and sometimes eggs, meat and fish. A visit to a farmers' market can even be a social event, a way to meet your neighbors and the farmers who supply your food. If you have kids, bring them along. Farmers' markets are kid-friendly and usually offers samples of what's in season.

Community Supported Agriculture (CSA)

Have the source come directly to you. Become a "member" of a local farm by buying a share of their annual yield. Boxes of seasonal produce and in some cases meat, eggs, and dairy products will be delivered (or available for pick-up) on a regular basis and are often less expensive than buying organic produce from grocery stores.

Grow Your Own

Whether you have space for just a few outdoor pots or a large plot of land, growing your own food is something to seriously consider. Almost nothing tastes better than a ripe, juicy homegrown tomato plucked from a vine right outside your door. More and more people, even city dwellers, are also starting to raise their own chickens for eggs. Grow, raise, fish, and hunt your own food and you'll never have to guess how it was treated and raised.

Foraging

Foraging for wild plants, nuts, and seeds has been key to the survival of the human species until fairly recently, when most of us stopped foraging and started buying food in stores. Modern-day food foraging is often less about survival and more about a desire to get closer to our food source and have a little adventure in the natural world. Some upscale restaurants now hire foragers to find interesting ingredients for the chef. Not all food in the wild, however, is fit to eat so before you bring home some wild greens or mushrooms it's wise to know exactly what it is you're eating. Spend time educating yourself, or better yet, sign up for a guided walk with an experienced forager.

STOCKING THE PRIMAL PANTRY

In addition to a wide variety of fresh vegetables, meat, seafood and select fruits that you'll buy regularly, it's helpful to have a pantry that is well stocked with less perishable staples. For both fresh ingredients and non-perishables, buy the most natural version you can, avoiding unnecessary ingredients, hormones, antibiotics and pesticides. Buy from local producers if possible, even for items like honey and nuts.

Here are a few key ingredients you'll want to keep on hand as you cook through the recipes in this book:

Herbs: Most fresh herbs will keep for up to a week if wrapped loosely in paper towels and stored in an airtight bag or plastic containers with tight lids in the refrigerator. Packed the same way, herbs can also be frozen for several months. Herbs with more delicate leaves, like cilantro and basil, tend to keep best outside of refrigeration in a jar of water. Herbs can also be dried. Tie them in bunches by the stem and hang them upside down in a cool, dry place for several weeks. After drying, pull the leaves off the herbs and store in airtight jars.

Spices: Most spices are sold in whole and ground form. Ideally, buy whole spices and grind them right before using—a coffee grinder reserved just for spices works well for this. Pre-ground spices tend to have less flavor and aromatics than whole spices. Either way, store spices away from heat, light and moisture. Every six months, think about replacing spices with fresh ones.

Healthy Fats and Oils: Our bodies need fat, and so do pretty much all recipes if you want them to taste good. It's good to have a few different types of cooking oils for different uses. Nut oils, avocado oil and higher quality (i.e. more expensive extra virgin olive oils) are best for flavoring food after it's cooked, rather than heating the oil up during the cooking process. Less expensive extra virgin olive oil and butter are good for sautéing and browning food at lower temperatures. Lard, coconut oil, ghee, clarified butter and unprocessed palm oil are good for high heat cooking and frying.

Nuts and Seeds: Staples for our cave-dwelling relations and good to have on hand in modern days, too. Ideally, buy raw nuts and seeds and roast them in your own oven at low heat if needed. Instead of stocking up on pre-made nut and seed butters, simply make your own by grinding nuts or seeds in a food processor with a little oil.

Sea Vegetables: Most forms of sea vegetables (i.e. kelp and seaweed) are dried and will keep in airtight packaging for months.

Broths: Consider making your own chicken, beef and vegetable broth and storing it in the freezer.

Non-Dairy Milks: Unsweetened coconut milk is used in many recipes in this cookbook. This canned milk keeps well for months in a cool pantry.

Flour Alternatives: Coconut flour, nut meal or nut flour are all good options.

Sweeteners: Although only used in moderation, maple syrup and raw honey are good to have on hand and keep for months.

THE PRIMAL KITCHEN

The single best way to improve the quality of your meals and "get Primal" is to choose and prepare food yourself. In your own Primal Kitchen you are in charge of the quality of ingredients. Therefore, you determine the quality of your food, and ultimately the positive or negative effect on your health and well-being. Cooking at home requires some advance planning and preparation, but is well worth it, especially when you have leftovers the next day to pack up for lunch. Here are some tips on how to become a tried and true Primal chef.

If you are a beginner in the kitchen, start by reading all the way through a recipe before you begin. Don't be put off by long ingredient lists, as they don't necessarily mean a recipe is going to be more difficult. Give yourself enough time to cook without feeling rushed. As you gain confidence in the kitchen you'll be amazed by how quickly you can get a meal on the table. Be prepared for some things to not turn out as expected and for some recipes to not match your palate. The more you cook, the more comfortable you will become with changing recipes to suit your personal tastes. If you are already comfortable in the kitchen, expand your experiences and try something new: add timeless techniques to your repertoire, such as preparing bone broths, long cooked roasts or homemade mayonnaise.

A well-equipped workspace saves time and effort in the long run, and can even take much of the drudgery out of meal preparation day after day, year after year. Kitchen tools and equipment come in a vast array of options, ranging from basic and manual to fully automatic with all the bells and whistles. You know the basics: sharp knives, cutting boards, spatulas, pots and pans, measuring cups and spoons, etc., but what about the tools and appliances that may not be a necessity? Here are a few of our favorite Primal Kitchen tools that will make life in the kitchen that much easier.

Dutch Oven or Casserole: A large, heavy, lidded pot that can be used on the stove and in the oven and is extremely handy for cooking large roasts or braising meat.

Handheld (stick) Immersion Blender: Blends ingredients right in a pot, bowl or other container. Use it to blend soup, batter, smoothies, etc.

Food Processor: For slicing, grating and chopping, as well as some mixing tasks. Some households will manage quite well with only a very small model, but a machine with an 11-cup bowl is the standard size and most convenient.

Thermometer (dial or digital): A thermometer takes the guess work out of cooking meat to desired doneness (rare, medium, well-done).

Slow Cooker: Otherwise known as a Crock-Pot, this appliance will slowly and safely cook meat and vegetables to unbelievable tenderness while you're busy doing something else.

Pressure Cooker: The opposite of a slow cooker. Cooks meat and vegetables in a fraction of the time it would take with traditional cooking methods. Ideal for cooking soups, stews and large cuts of meat.

Mandoline: Slices fruits and vegetables into extremely thin and symmetrical shapes. Great for making zucchini noodles and vegetable chips and for making salads more interesting.

Dehydrator: Dries fruit and vegetables and can even be used to make jerky.

RECIPES

MEAT

Meat is a concentrated source of protein and nutrients, not to mention a tasty and satisfying part of any meal. The recipes in this chapter range from simple, juicy steaks to shanks seasoned with an array of aromatic spices and braised in a silky coconut sauce. Some of the recipes take hours of cooking and are perfect for weekend meals; some recipes take no time at all and can easily be thrown together on busy weeknights.

Each of the recipes suggest a specific type of meat that will go well with the seasonings, but let the recipes be a guide, not a strict set of instructions. The type of meat you use for each recipe should be determined by what you crave, as well as by what is available from your butcher, or what you already have in your freezer.

Meat That's Fit to Eat

The combination of hormones, antibiotics and fortified grains most mass-produced animals are raised on (not to mention their objectionable living conditions) makes conventionally raised animals less than ideal. There is no question that the modern system of concentrated feedlots is an affront to both our health and our desire to live harmoniously with nature. Hunting and butchering your own meat would be ideal, but isn't realistic for most of us. So what is a compassionate omnivore to do?

Buying the entire animal directly from the farm—or at least in portions after divvying it up with friends—is a good way for anyone with the proper motivation to understand their meat.

Go Organic

Certified organic meat comes from animals that are humanely raised and fed grass or grain feed without hormones, antibiotics, sewage sludge, genetic engineering or artificial ingredients. Yes, organic meat is more expensive, but think of it as an investment in your health. Mitigate the cost by choosing less expensive "thrift cuts".

Buy From Local Producers

Visit AmericanGrassFedBeef.com and EatWild.com to find local meat producers.

There is peace of mind that comes from knowing exactly where and how your meat has been produced. As an added bonus, the meat bought directly from a small farm should be incredibly fresh and flavorful. Talk to owners of small farms in your region and you're likely to find out that although they aren't certified organic (a costly and lengthy process) they do follow sustainable and organic guidelines. While individual cuts of meat from local producers may not always be more economical, buying the entire animal and sharing the cost of the meat with others can be. This practice of sharing the meat from a whole animal has become so popular that it's officially entered the culinary lexicon as…

Cowpooling

Buying sides of beef or whole butchered hogs from small producers will provide you with healthy, clean meat and can end up being less per pound than organic meat purchased at grocery stores. Talk to neighbors, friends and family members about sharing the cost and divvying up the meat. If you eat meat regularly and have a large freezer, cowpooling is for you. Visit your local farmers' market or go online to find out more about producers in your area that you can purchase from.

GRILLED STEAK

Properly grilling a good steak is a skill all Primal meat eaters should perfect. Grilled steak is quick and easy to prepare, has little waste, and remains a familiar favorite for many people. When you make steak, try to have the majority of your dinner already prepped and ready to serve to avoid last minute distraction and possibly overcooking the meat.

INSTRUCTIONS:

Defrost steaks (if frozen) in a shallow dish in the refrigerator (may take 1–2 days) covered, or in a plastic bag in a bowl of cold water (for a few hours).

Pat steaks dry with a paper towel. Rub both sides of steak with salt and pepper. Let the steaks sit at room temperature to take the chill off while the grill preheats.

INGREDIENTS:

Steaks 1–1 ½ inches thick, from tender cuts (NY Strip/Top Loin, Rib or Ribeye, Tenderloin/Filet Mignon, Sirloin/Sirloin Tip, Top Round, London Broil, Tri-Tip, T-bone, Porterhouse)

Coarse sea salt and freshly ground black pepper to taste

Minced garlic and herbs *(optional)*

Gas Grills: Turn gas on high to burn off residual cooking debris and grease while preheating. Use a wire BBQ grate brush if necessary to remove sticky or thick residue. Turn one gas burner down to medium-high setting and turn all other burners off.

Charcoal Grills: Light charcoal and burn until briquettes are covered with ash and glowing inside. Using a long handled BBQ tool, rake hot coals to one side to create a direct heat side and an indirect heat side.

Place steaks to sear on preheated grill grates over the direct heat for about 2–3 minutes, with lid closed. To make attractive grill marks and prevent sticking, avoid moving steaks once they hit the grill.

Open lid and use tongs to flip steaks. Cook second side about 2–3 minutes.

Move steaks to a grill area over the indirect heat side, close the lid and leave undisturbed until steaks are 120–140°F internal temperature (rare to medium-rare). Depending on steak thickness, this usually takes about 10–25 minutes. Use a thermometer or the "touch" method to determine doneness.

When done, remove steaks to a warmed platter, cover with a piece of foil (tented) for 5–10 minutes, so the juices will redistribute within the meat. If you cut into the meat too early, you'll lose too much juice.

Less tender cuts such as the London Broil, Top Round, and sometimes Sirloin are best cut into thin slices across the grain before serving.

The "Touch" Method

Determine meat doneness like a grilling professional—press the meat surface lightly and quickly with your index fingertip. If the steak feels soft like your cheek hollow, it is cooked rare; if it feels like your chin pad, it's medium-rare; if it is firm like your nose-tip, it's cooked medium; if it is very firm like your forehead, it's well done and you've overcooked your steak.

PRIMAL POT ROAST

Pot roast is old-fashioned comfort food that is nearly forgotten in today's rush for 30 minute "almost homemade" convenience gimmicks, but this classic roast can fit well into the modern Primal Blueprint lifestyle with just a small amount of kitchen time spread out over several hours—perfect for a weekend morning or afternoon at home. Pot roast can even be cooked in advance, then chilled or frozen for reheating later on a busy weeknight—the flavor improves in a day or two. Pot roast is easy on the budget and makes enough servings for larger families or multiple days' meals. Pot roast is delicious served with puréed cauliflower or parsnips.

INGREDIENTS:

Seasoning rub:
1 teaspoon dried thyme
1 teaspoon dried crushed rosemary
1 tablespoon paprika
1 tablespoon coarse sea salt
1 teaspoon freshly ground black pepper

1 4-pound beef or bison chuck

2 tablespoons home rendered lard, tallow, ghee, or olive oil

1 cup water, beef or chicken stock or dry red wine (might not use it all)

3 large onions, thinly sliced
6 garlic cloves, coarsely chopped

SERVINGS: 6 or more

INSTRUCTIONS:

Combine the seasoning rub ingredients in a small bowl then rub the meat well with the seasonings. For the best flavor, let the roast sit out an hour or two at room temperature, loosely covered with foil, or well-wrapped overnight in the refrigerator.

Preheat the oven to 350°F (325°F for bison).

In a Dutch oven or a large heavy casserole, heat the fat over medium-high heat. Brown the roast on all sides, about 2 minutes per side. Remove the roast temporarily to a plate or platter. Remove excess fat that has accumulated in the pan (bison will render nearly no fat). Add water, stock or wine to the pan and deglaze by scraping and dissolving the brown bits on the bottom. Return the roast to the pan, cover it with the sliced onions and garlic, cover and bake in the oven for one hour.

How to Keep Frozen Meat Fresh

Knowing how to properly freeze meat lets you take advantage of sales at the butcher shop and plan ahead for future meals. To avoid freezer burn, remove the meat from all of its original store packaging, dry with a thick paper towel to remove excess moisture, then tightly wrap in cling film, being sure all sides are secure and covered. Repeat the cling film wrap, this time wrapping from the open side first and then store in a plastic zipper bag (with all air removed). While this might seem a little extreme, we promise you that following this process will ensure that you will never again throw out a cut of meat!

[Primal Pot Roast cont'd]

Remove the cover, turn the roast and continue to cook in the oven **uncovered**, for another hour. Add more liquid if needed and stir the onions a bit after 30 minutes for even cooking.

Cover again and cook one hour more. The meat will be done when it is fork-tender. Remove the meat from the pot and let it rest, loosely covered with foil.

Strain the sauce, de-fatting if necessary. Season sauce with salt and pepper if desired. If there is a shoulder bone, remove it. Slice the meat or separate it into chunks for serving. Serve sauce over the meat after plating.

To reheat, place meat in casserole or pan with a bit of leftover sauce, or 2–3 tablespoons water or broth. Cover with lid or foil and bake at 325°F, or on the range at medium-low heat until heated through, about 15–20 minutes.

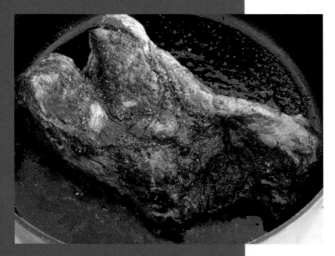

Note: Pot Roast may also be made in a slow cooker. Brown meat in a large skillet on the stove, then place the meat in the crock. Place the onions on top of the meat and pour liquid over all. Cook covered on LOW for 7–8 hours. Remove cooked meat to a warm platter (be careful, it may fall apart into chunks) and cover with foil to retain heat. Strain liquid (onions may be placed on the meat if desired or left in the sauce) and simmer in a saucepan on the range over medium-heat until reduced by half. Pour some sauce on the meat and pass the remaining sauce in a gravy boat at the table.

Slow Cooker Italian Pot Roast

Rich balsamic vinegar and a small section of oxtail give this pot roast a very rich and savory flavor. Get it started the night before, or in the morning for a stress-free dinner. This is an excellent recipe for a dinner party.

INGREDIENTS:

4 pounds chuck roast, removed from refrigeration 1 hour before cooking

3 or 4 inch section of oxtail *(optional, but it really makes a difference in the sauce flavor and texture)*

2 tablespoons fat
1 large onion, chopped
2 cloves garlic, crushed

4 inch sprig fresh rosemary (or 1 teaspoon dried)

1 cup water, beef or chicken stock, or dry red wine

¼ cup balsamic vinegar
2 cups finely chopped tomatoes

S E R V I N G S: 6 with leftovers

I N S T R U C T I O N S:

Warm a few tablespoons of fat or oil in a big, heavy skillet and brown the chuck roast on all sides. Put the section of oxtail in the bottom of the slow cooker. Put the roast on top of the oxtail. Add the onion, garlic, rosemary on top of the beef.

Add water, stock or wine to the pan and deglaze by scraping and dissolving the brown bits on the bottom. Add the liquid to the slow cooker, along with the balsamic vinegar and tomatoes.

Don't Shock the Meat

Meat that goes directly from a cold refrigerator to a hot pan has a hard time adjusting to the extreme temperature change and won't cook evenly or in the amount of time a recipe suggests. Before you cook meat, let it sit out (covered, of course) for at least a half hour. This is enough time for the meat to come up in temperature so it will cook evenly, but it is too short a time to promote any significant bacteria growth due to lack of refrigeration.

[Slow Cooker Italian Pot Roast cont'd]

Cook covered on low setting for 8 hours. Remove roast to a warmed serving platter. Strain the liquid, discarding the oxtail bones and rosemary stem (leave the leaves), then place remaining onions and tomatoes on top of the roast. Cover the roast with foil to retain heat.

Simmer strained liquid until reduced by half—it will be rich and flavorful due to the oxtail section that cooked along with it.

Spoon some of the reduced sauce over the roast and pass the rest of the sauce in a gravy dish at the table.

SHANKS A LOT, BRUCE
(OR, BRAISED BEEF SHANKS WITH COCONUT MILK, GINGER, AND CUMIN)

This is a spin on a favorite Bruce Aidell recipe. Just a few tweaks, like eliminating the flour and substituting bison shanks for beef, make this delicious recipe quite Primal.

Don't let the long list of ingredients fool you; this is really simple to put together. The Eastern spices are really aromatic and the coconut milk adds a silky richness to the braising sauce. If you don't have coriander, turmeric, and cumin, substitute curry powder instead.

This oven braised dish could easily be transformed into a slow cooker recipe, too. Simply brown the meat, use about one-third less beef stock and coconut milk, and cook it on the low setting for 6–8 hours (4–6 hours on high).

SERVINGS: 4

INSTRUCTIONS:

Preheat oven to 325°F. In a large roasting pan or a Dutch oven, melt half the ghee or coconut oil over medium-high heat. Add the vegetables, the garlic, and the ginger, lower the heat to medium and cook about 10 minutes, stirring occasionally. Remove the vegetables to a bowl and keep warm.

Season the meat with salt and pepper. Add the remaining ghee or coconut oil to the pan and heat. Over medium-high heat, brown the meat until all sides are well-browned, about 5–10 minutes. Remove meat to a plate.

Reduce the heat and add the coriander, cumin, turmeric, and red pepper flakes, stirring to release the oils and aromas

INGREDIENTS:

5 tablespoons ghee (clarified butter) or coconut oil, divided use

2 cups chopped onion
2 carrots, cut into small dice
2 cloves garlic, minced
1 tablespoon minced fresh ginger

2 teaspoons coarse sea salt, plus more to taste

1 teaspoon freshly ground black pepper

About 3 pounds bison shanks, cut into pieces 1 ½ to 2 inches thick

2 teaspoons ground coriander
1 teaspoon ground cumin
½ teaspoon turmeric
½ teaspoon red pepper flakes
1 ½ cups beef stock
1 can (14 ounces) unsweetened coconut milk
1 cinnamon stick
3 cardamom pods, lightly smashed
2 bay leaves
Chopped fresh cilantro for garnish

[Shanks A Lot, Bruce cont'd]

while they "toast". Add half the beef stock to deglaze the pan, scraping up the browned bits on the bottom of the pan. Add the rest of the beef stock and the coconut milk and bring to a boil.

Wrap the cinnamon stick, cardamom pods and bay leaves in an herb bag (a stapled cone-shaped coffee filter works, too) and add the pouch of spices to the liquid. Return the meat and vegetables to the pan, including any juices that may have accumulated. Cover, bring to a boil and place in the preheated oven. Braise for 2 ½ to 3 ½ hours until the meat is tender and pulling away from the bone.

When cooking is finished, remove shanks to a heated platter and cover with foil to retain heat. Reduce the sauce over medium heat to slightly thicken. Remove spice pouch and adjust salt and pepper as necessary.

Serve the shanks over cauliflower rice "couscous" **(see recipe on page 184)** with sauce, garnished with cilantro.

Gee, What is Ghee?

Originated in India, ghee is butter that has been melted slowly over low heat until the milk solids sink to the bottom of the pan and a golden liquid rises to the top. Any foam that rises to the top as well is skimmed off and the pure, golden butter fat that remains is ghee. Without any milk solids in it, ghee has a higher smoke point than regular butter which makes it a good choice for sautéing and frying.

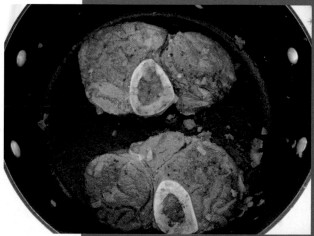

CARDIFF CRACK

A small neighborhood sea-side market in Cardiff-by-the-Sea, California is known for its marinated tri-tip roast, which is officially called Burgundy Pepper Tri-Tip. The locals call it "Cardiff Crack", and with good reason. The actual marinade they use in the store is a closely guarded secret, but this is a close approximation.

Tri-tip is a relatively tender cut at a reasonable price (good); it's an easy piece of meat to pick up on the way home to grill for dinner (great); and oh, yeah, it's addictive (oh boy!). Tri-tip tends to be a Western region cut, so you might have to ask the butcher if he can cut one for you if you are in another part of the country. Sirloin Tip Roast or London Broil are good substitutes, too.

INGREDIENTS:

1 to 2 cups dry red wine (even the leftover half bottle in the back of the fridge will do)

¼ cup extra virgin olive oil
3 cloves minced garlic
1 teaspoon honey

1 tablespoon (or more!) fresh ground black pepper

INSTRUCTIONS:

Mix marinade ingredients together in a plastic zip bag, then add the tri-tip roast. Seal, pressing out excess air so all sides of meat are covered with marinade. Chill for at least several hours or overnight in the refrigerator.

Remove roast from marinade bag and blot dry with a paper towel. Let roast sit out 15–20 minutes to take the chill off.

Meanwhile prepare grill for direct heat on one side and indirect heat on the other side (see recipe for Grilled Steak on page 13).

Grill over high heat for 5–7 minutes on each side. Move to indirect heat and cook for an additional 10 minutes each side—or until interior temperature reaches 125–130°F (medium-rare).

Let sit loosely covered with foil for an additional 10 minutes. Temperature will continue to rise as much as 10 more degrees. Cut against the grain into thin

Going Against The Grain

Look closely at that piece of meat. You'll notice a pattern in the meat—muscle strands that are known as the meat grain. Slicing meat in the same direction as the grain will yield tough, chewy meat but cutting diagonally through the meat grain, either before or after cooking, will produce tender slices.

[Cardiff Crack cont'd]

slices. Spoon juice over meat when serving. Leftovers make great lunches, especially with big tossed salads.

DELI-STYLE ROAST BEEF

Sliced rare or medium-rare, deli roast beef is a great convenience food for easy meals and snacks, but who wants the additives often found in commercial roast beef? Making your own at home is easier than you think.

SERVINGS: Varies, depending on the size of the roast. Approximately one-third to one-half pound per serving.

INSTRUCTIONS:

Combine the garlic, herbs, salt, and pepper in a small bowl. Rub the meat well with seasoning mix, coating all exterior surfaces of the roast. For the best flavor and even cooking, let the roast sit out two hours at room temperature, loosely wrapped in a plastic zip bag.

Preheat the oven to 250°F.

INGREDIENTS:

1 roast (beef, bison, venison) from the round or sirloin (tri-tip cut is especially good)

2 garlic cloves, minced
1 tablespoon dried crushed rosemary
2 tablespoons dried oregano
1 ½ tablespoons coarse sea salt
2 teaspoons freshly ground pepper

Place the meat in a small roasting pan and insert a meat thermometer (with the tip in the center of the roast at the thickest part), and cook for half an hour.

Turn the temperature down as low as the oven will go (170°, 160°F, 150°F is even better). Continue cooking until meat is very rare (120–125°F), rare (130°F), or medium-rare (135–140°F). More well done than this will not yield good results with these lean cuts. Grass-fed bison and wild venison will cook quicker than beef because they are extremely lean and don't have the internal marbling that grain fed beef has.

Remove roast from the oven, cover loosely with foil, and rest for 10 minutes. Cut into the thinnest possible slices with a very sharp slicing knife and serve warm. For authentic deli-style roast beef, cool 20 minutes longer on the counter, then chill several hours in the refrigerator in an airtight container. Slice into very thin slices, using a very sharp slicing knife. An electric meat slicer is even better as it make extremely thin slices. Only slice off what you can use each time, because the larger roast has less exposed surface area for oxidation and will keep better than the slices, at least several days to a week.

BISON CHILI

Chili is simple to prepare and is a very good recipe to make on the weekend while tending to household chores in between cooking steps. Be sure to make enough for leftovers as chili reheats well and perhaps even tastes better after the spices meld during a night or two in the refrigerator.

This is a delicious meat-based chili (bean-free); very rich and flavorful due to the touch of bacon and its fat, the long simmering time, and the addition of a secret ingredient, cocoa powder.

Chili also is easy to scale up or down in servings, and is economical when feeding a crowd. This version of chili is not very spicy; feel free to add more spice or hot pepper to taste. It can also be made with ground beef, preferably grass-fed. Grass-fed bison and beef are quite lean and should never be cooked over high heat temps.

INGREDIENTS:

2–3 slices of uncooked bacon, chopped or 24 ounces of finely chopped pancetta (Italian bacon)

1 onion, chopped
4 cloves garlic, coarsely chopped

2 pounds ground bison (grass-fed beef may be substituted)

2 tablespoons chili powder

1 teaspoon dried oregano or 1 tablespoon fresh minced oregano

1 teaspoon paprika
1 1/2–2 cups water (or beef broth)

1 14.5-ounce can finely chopped tomatoes with liquid (28 ounce can may be used also) or 3–4 medium size tomatoes, seeded and diced

1 tablespoon unsweetened cocoa powder
1 tablespoon apple cider vinegar

1–2 peeled carrots, cut into 1/2 inch dice or smaller (optional)

Optional garnishes: finely chopped avocado, chopped cilantro, grated cheese, sour cream or crème fraîche

Bison—The Perfect Primal Meat

Bison, or American buffalo, has changed little since the days when it roamed the Great Plains of North America in massive herds and was hunted by Native Americans. Nearly driven to extinction during Westward Expansion in the 19th century, bison herd populations have been making a comeback in recent years and are sustainably raised by numerous small family ranches throughout Western North America. Naturally lean and higher in protein (by weight) than beef, grass-fed bison has an excellent ratio of omega-3 to omega-6 fatty acids.

[Bison Chili cont'd]

SERVINGS: 6

INSTRUCTIONS:

In a large saucepan (at least 4 quart size) or Dutch oven, over medium-low heat, cook bacon or pancetta a few minutes until slightly brown and some fat is rendered out.

Add chopped onion to the pan and stir into bacon. When the onions are semi-translucent, add garlic and stir. Cook a few minutes longer. Add ground meat to pan and cook over medium-low heat until brown (cooked) throughout and no pink remains. If fat seems insufficient, add some saved bacon drippings, lard, or olive oil to keep bison meat from sticking to the pan and drying out. If higher fat ground beef is used, it might be necessary to collect some fat in a large spoon and remove it.

Add spices, water or broth, tomatoes and carrots and stir well to combine. Cover and simmer over low heat for one hour, stirring every 20 minutes or so to prevent sticking (adjust temperature up or down a bit as necessary to keep chili simmering, but not sticking to the bottom of the pan).

Add vinegar and cocoa powder and stir well, adding additional water if necessary, then simmer uncovered another 20 minutes. Taste and season with sea salt and black pepper, to taste.

If more spicy "heat" is desired, add hot pepper sauce to the pot or to individual servings at the table.

Suggestions for leftover chili:

Reheat leftover chili (adding a few tablespoons of water if necessary) in a pan on the stove and serve over hot steamed cauliflower florets. Or, stretch a small amount of leftover chili by making a serving of soup: heat one cup of beef or chicken broth or coconut milk with added carrot chunks, cauliflower florets, or finely chopped tomatoes until vegetables are 'fork tender'. Add leftover chili and stir. Garnish with finely chopped avocado and/or chopped cilantro.

SAUSAGE STEW

The original recipe that inspired this stew made enough to feed an army, so this one is scaled down considerably. Feel free to reduce it by half or double it as needed; stews and soups are rather flexible. The amount of broth determines if this turns out more soup-like or stew-like.

You could also call this recipe Clean-Out-The-Fridge Stew. The beauty of the recipe is that it doesn't have to be the same each time it is made; use this recipe as a starting point and add what you have on hand. Any combination of leftover bits of meat works (especially pork) and "orphans of the veggie drawer" are put to good use—limp celery, forgotten carrots. Voluminous bunches of miscellaneous CSA greens can be put to good use with this recipe, too.

The first time I made this I didn't have any broth available, but I did have a pig foot (trotter) in the freezer, something I'd been meaning to use. The trotter was perfectly suited and made a rich, delicious broth. Check your local farmers' markets or Latino "mercado de carne" for pig feet; a ham hock would work well, too. These oft-neglected bony cuts don't provide a lot of meat, but when simmered the bones and rich gelatinous connective tissues create a nourishing and flavorful broth, especially if you add a bit of vinegar to acidify the water and facilitate movement of minerals from the bones into the broth.

INGREDIENTS:

1 ½ to 2 ½ quarts beef or chicken broth (or use water and a split pig foot or ham hock)

1 tablespoon cider vinegar (if using water and pig foot or ham hock instead of broth)

Approximately 1 pound leftover meat (any combination of pork, ham, beef, lamb, etc.), coarsely chopped

1 onion, coarsely chopped
2 ribs celery, coarsely chopped
1 carrot, coarsely chopped

¼ head of cabbage, sliced or coarsely chopped

1 pound Italian sweet sausage (if links, cut into 1 inch rounds; if sausage is loose, form into 1 inch balls or chunks)

1 head cauliflower, cut into florets

1 bunch (about 1 pound) washed greens (chard, kale, turnip, collard, etc.), coarsely chopped

½ head of garlic, peeled, trimmed, and coarsely chopped

2 tablespoon chopped fresh basil or Italian flat leaf parsley (or 1 teaspoon dried)

Salt and freshly ground pepper, to taste

S E R V I N G S: 6–8

I N S T R U C T I O N S:

Heat broth in a stockpot or a Dutch oven. If using water and a pig foot or ham hock instead of broth, bring the water to a boil and add the foot or hock and vinegar. Lower heat and simmer about 45 minutes to an hour, uncovered, to make broth. If foot or hock remains intact, leave it in. If it is falling apart, remove with tongs or a slotted spoon.

Add chopped meat to hot broth and simmer for 1 hour, uncovered. Add onion, celery, carrots and cabbage and simmer for 20 minutes more.

Cook the sausage chunks in a large skillet and brown for 10 minutes over medium heat to render some of the fat and develop flavor. Add the sausage to the soup pot with the cauliflower, greens, garlic, and basil or parsley and cook for an additional 10 minutes or until all the vegetables and meats are tender. Add salt and pepper to taste. If pig foot or hock still remain in the stew, remove and discard if desired.

GRANDMA'S EASY BBQ PORK

This recipe has been handed down in one of our reader's families for at least three generations. Anna's very healthy 90-year-old grandmother reports that she clipped the recipe from a magazine more than 60 years ago. It isn't a really authentic BBQ sauce, though the vinegary flavor is reminiscent of North Carolina-style BBQ sauce. The rich sauce was traditionally served with boiled or mashed potatoes or rice, but mashed cauliflower, turnips, or parsnips soak up the sauce very nicely as a side, as does shredded cabbage.

The preparation of this dish is very easy and fast (even if you have to make a batch of ketchup first), but the long baking time in the oven makes it an excellent recipe to prepare for company so you can attend to other tasks. The meat can be kept warm in a covered casserole in the oven after the cooking time is up without fear of overcooking; the pork meat just becomes more "fall-apart" tender. Feel free to half or double the recipe, changing the size of the cooking vessel if it seems necessary.

SERVINGS: 8 or more

INSTRUCTIONS:

Preheat oven to 325°F.

Brown meat on all sides in fat/oil over medium to medium-high heat in a flame-proof casserole or Dutch oven.

While the meat is browning, combine remaining ingredients and stir to mix well.

When meat has browned, remove from heat and pour mixture over the meat.

INGREDIENTS:

1 tablespoon olive oil or high quality lard

8 pork chops or about 4 pounds of pork shoulder roast, use bone-in chops or a bone-in shoulder roast instead of boneless for the richest tasting sauce

1 small onion, finely chopped

½ cup ketchup (see page 234 for "Primal 51 Ketchup" recipe)

1 cup water
⅓ cup vinegar
1 teaspoon salt
1 teaspoon celery seed
½ teaspoon nutmeg
1 bay leaf

Cover with lid or foil and bake at 325°F for 1 ½ hours for chops and about 2 ½ hours for roast. Check halfway through baking time, adding a small amount of additional water if necessary.

Remove bay leaf, transfer chops or roast to a warm platter and pour sauce in a gravy boat or pitcher. Spoon or pour some sauce over the meat to moisten.

SMOKED SAUSAGE AND CABBAGE

This is a really simple, satisfying comfort dish that is great on a busy day when you need to keep it simple, and want to sit down in under an hour. Young kids can help hone their knife skills on the sausage while you make short work of the cabbage with a sharp knife and cutting board. It will work with turkey kielbasa if you use a little more fat to compensate for the lack of fat from the sausage.

INGREDIENTS:

1 smoked kielbasa sausage ring, cut into ¾ inch slices

1 head cabbage, thinly sliced (or one large bag of precut cabbage)

1 or 2 tablespoons of water or broth

2 tablespoons bacon fat, olive oil, or ghee

SERVINGS: 4

INSTRUCTIONS:

Preheat the oven to 350°F.

Grease the bottom and halfway up the sides of an ovenproof casserole with some of the fat. Add the cabbage, water or broth. Place the sliced kielbasa sausage on top of the cabbage. Dot the cabbage in a few places with some more fat, then cover with a lid or foil and place it in the oven for approximately 40 minutes, removing the cover in the last 10 minutes so it will brown a little on top.

Transylvanian Stockpot

This recipe is great for late fall or winter when a hearty soup seems just right. Why is it called Transylvanian Stockpot? Well, it's just one of those family recipes that has always gone by that name and we've never wanted to tinker with a good thing.

INGREDIENTS:

6 ounces bacon, cut crosswise into 1 inch pieces (or same amount of finely chopped pancetta)

1 large onion, thinly sliced or chopped
3 cloves garlic, coarsely chopped

1 small green cabbage (or ½ large), cored, cut into wedges, then sliced

1 tablespoon paprika, hot or mild

½ teaspoon freshly ground black pepper

1 can (28 ounces) finely chopped tomatoes or 3 fresh tomatoes, seeded and diced

3 cups chicken broth

1 cinnamon stick or 1 teaspoon ground cinnamon (or both)

⅓ cup golden raisins
2 bay leaves

1 pound smoked kielbasa Polish sausage, sliced into thin rounds

Handful of chopped parsley

Optional garnish: crème fraîche, sour cream, or plain Greek-style strained whole milk yogurt

SERVINGS: 6

INSTRUCTIONS:

In a large heavy non-reactive pot, cook bacon or pancetta over medium heat until bacon begins to crisp, stirring every few minutes. Add onion and garlic, sautéing until onions wilt and are translucent (reduce heat if necessary to avoid burning garlic, which will in turn create a bitter flavor).

Add cabbage, paprika, and black pepper and stir to mix. Cook about 5 minutes, stirring a few times.

Add tomatoes with their juice, broth, cinnamon, raisins, and bay leaves. Raise heat to medium-high, stir, and bring to a boil. Reduce heat, cover, and simmer about 45 minutes.

Add sliced kielbasa and heat through. Stir in chopped parsley.

Ladle into wide, shallow bowls. Garnish with chopped flat leaf parsley and a dollop of crème fraîche, sour cream, or plain whole milk yogurt *(optional)*.

BAKIN' BACON

This is the hands-down easiest and cleanest way to cook bacon, but it isn't the fastest by a long shot, so plan ahead. The cooked strips will lay flat and be evenly cooked.

You can also remove the bacon when cooked about two-thirds through, rendering out most of the grease. Then chill or freeze the bacon strips in wax-paper layers for a quick finish or reheat later. Precooking is a great time saver for busy mornings, or while camping and grilling outside, as it is more efficient and reduces clean-up and flare-up problems that can accompany large amounts of dangerous hot grease. At the low temperature of 250°F, the bacon grease will not splatter and soil the oven, but instead will drip slowly through the rack and collect in the bottom of the sheet pan for easier cleanup.

INSTRUCTIONS:

Preheat oven to 250°F.

Place a flat cooling rack inside a large sheet pan. Place slices of bacon on rack, evenly spaced and close together but not overlapping or bunched up. Quantity to be baked is only limited by number of oven racks and pans.

Place pan of bacon in oven and bake. Check on bacon after one hour and then every 20–30 minutes, until bacon reaches desired level of chewiness or crispness. Depending on bacon thickness, fat-to-meat ratio, and moisture content, it may take an average of about 2 hours to achieve crisp bacon, less time for chewier bacon.

Bacon fat may be strained through a very fine steel mesh strainer and chilled for later use (bacon fat mayonnaise!).

Pulled or Chopped Pork Shoulder BBQ

BBQ pork shoulder is a crowd pleasing favorite budget cut of meat and quite simple and easy to make provided you have ample time—at least 8 hours, and sometimes up to 10 if the roast is very large or you are cooking more than one. You don't want to rush pork shoulder because those muscles do a lot of work and need the long, slow cooking method to slow melt the collagen in the connective tissue and baste the meat with the natural fat. When the meat is done, it will easily pull apart into succulent shreds.

Use soaked and drained hickory wood chips if you have the time to replenish them hourly and want authentic BBQ aroma and flavor, but it's quite delicious without the wood smoke, too.

INGREDIENTS:

2 tablespoons chili powder
2 tablespoons coarse sea salt
1 to 2 tablespoons granulated garlic
2 teaspoons freshly ground black pepper
1 teaspoon dry mustard
3–6 pound pork shoulder roast with some fat on the outside, bone-in or boneless (tied together with butcher string if boneless)
Soaked and drained hickory wood chips *(optional)*

SERVINGS: 4–6

INSTRUCTIONS:

Pat the pork shoulder dry with a paper towel and place in a flat pan.

Mix together the dry ingredients for the dry rub and apply to the pork shoulder roast, coating all surfaces and rubbing in well. Let roast sit at room temperature for 20–30 minutes to take the chill off. Insert a remote temperature probe into the center of the roast if you wish to monitor the temperature. If the shoulder bone is intact, make sure the thermometer is not touching it (it will give inaccurate readings).

What's The Rub

Save time and effort: Make up a double or triple batch of the dry rub. Store in an airtight jar at room temperature and use on steak or roasts.

[Pulled or Chopped Pork Shoulder BBQ cont'd]

Prepare the grill or smoker for indirect low heat to achieve a temperature of about 225–250°F (place an oven thermometer on the grill rack next to the roast). Slowly cook the roast over indirect heat (covered with the lid) for 8–10 hours, maintaining a constant temperature of 225–250°F. Replenish hot coals periodically if using that method. Soaked and drained hickory wood chips may be added to the coals or smoker box at the beginning and again every hour if a smoky flavor and aroma is desired. Cook until the roast reaches an internal temperature of 190°F and is falling apart tender in some parts.

Transfer to a sheet pan, wrap the roast well with foil, and let it rest for about 30 minutes.

Unwrap the roast and pull the meat apart with two forks, your fingers, or chop into ½ inch pieces on a cutting board, then place in a warm bowl. Remove any tough sinew or large layers of fat.

Alternative cooking technique:

Pulled pork may also be cooked in a slow cooker on low setting for 7–8 hours with excellent results. However, it will not have the smokiness that a grill or smoker provides. Skip the wrapping in foil step and after shredding/chopping, mix some of the juices that accumulated in the slow cooker with the meat before serving. Or, smoke or grill the roast over indirect heat for about 3–4 hours, then transfer to a covered baking vessel in a 325°F oven for another 2–3 hours.

ROASTED LEG OF LAMB WITH HERBS AND GARLIC

The mild flavor of lamb is always made more interesting when embellished generously with herbs and garlic. The combination of herbs can be adjusted according to what you have on hand or in your garden. Parsley, sage, lavender and oregano all pair well with lamb. If you're cooking a larger leg, double the herb rub and extend the cooking time until the desired temperature is reached.

Lamb is especially prone to turning tough if overcooked. The key to tender lamb is serving it when it's still pink and leaning towards rare. Use a meat thermometer and remove the lamb from the oven when it reaches between 125–135°F. Let the lamb rest for 10–20 minutes and the temperature should rise another 10 degrees. The range for medium-rare falls anywhere between 130 (more pink) and 140 (less pink) degrees Fahrenheit.

SERVINGS: 6

INSTRUCTIONS:

Preheat oven to 350°F.

In a food processor or blender, mix olive oil with garlic, lemon zest, tablespoon of rosemary and tablespoon of thyme. Cut small slits on top of lamb and rub the whole lamb thoroughly with herb mixture. Heat a large pan and brown the lamb on all sides (3–6 minutes a side). Remove the lamb and add broth, scraping up any browned bits still in the pan and stirring them into broth.

INGREDIENTS:

2 ½ to 3 pound boneless leg of lamb, removed from refrigeration at least a half hour before cooking

3 tablespoons olive oil
3 garlic cloves (or more)
Zest of 1 lemon

1 tablespoon fresh rosemary, plus 10 or so sprigs

1 tablespoon fresh thyme, plus 10 or so sprigs

4 bay leaves
½ cup chicken or beef broth
1 pound mushrooms

[Roasted Leg of Lamb with Herbs and Garlic cont'd]

In a large casserole pan, lay the sprigs of rosemary and thyme and the bay leaves down and set lamb on top. Surround with whole mushrooms (other vegetables of your choice can be added as well.) Add broth. Roast approximately 45 minutes or until the lamb registers between 125–135°F on a meat thermometer. Remove from oven, loosely cover with foil, and let sit 10–20 minutes. Slice thinly before serving.

Where Does Your Lamb Live?

As a lamb matures and becomes mutton (a sheep aged 1 year or older) it has a stronger, gamier taste and may also have a more grainy texture. Where a lamb comes from and what type of breed it is can also affect the flavor and texture. New Zealand lamb tends to be leaner and have a stronger flavor. Australian lamb typically has more fat and a less pronounced flavor. Icelandic lamb is thought to be the most tender and delicately flavored. Lamb raised in the US tends to be fattier (often due to a diet of corn before slaughter) and the flavor ranges from mild to gamey. Look to farmers' markets and local producers for domestic lamb that is entirely grass-fed.

Five Spice Beef and Broccoli Stir Fry

Chinese five spice powder is a blend of ground cinnamon, cloves, fennel seeds, star anise and peppercorns that can be found in most grocery stores. This warm blend goes especially well with beef and gives the stir fry a complex flavor that is slightly sweet, smoky and earthy. A little bit of five spice powder goes a long way—all you need is a pinch.

INGREDIENTS:

½ pound flank or skirt steak
3 tablespoons wheat-free tamari
1 tablespoon sesame oil
¼ teaspoon Chinese five spice powder
2 teaspoon grated ginger
1 garlic clove, minced
1 head of broccoli, cut in florets and steamed
6 ounces (a few big handfuls) mung bean sprouts
¼ cup finely chopped mint
¼ cup finely chopped cilantro

SERVINGS: 2–4

INSTRUCTIONS:

Mix together a marinade of tamari, oil, five spice powder, ginger and garlic. Slice the meat into thin strips. Marinate at least 15 minutes or up to several hours if you have time. Heat a sauté pan or wok. Add meat and marinade to the pan and sauté 3–5 minutes, stirring a few times so the meat cooks evenly. Add broccoli and sauté a few more minutes. Add mung bean sprouts and remove from heat. Garnish with fresh herbs.

OFFAL

For some, eating offal requires that they gather a little bit of courage beforehand. For others, it's a favorite delicacy or a standard of their youth (liver and onions, anyone?). Organ meats often have a flavor that is milder than people expect. The real challenge is knowing how to cook them, so we've laid out several very simple recipes in this chapter.

While offal isn't for everyone, it is a primal food that's typically affordable and has numerous health benefits. If you've ever thought of delving into offal, now is your chance. Start with something more familiar, like liver, then work your way up to sweetbreads.

STEAK AND KIDNEY STEW

This is a wheat and gluten-free variation on the classic British Steak and Kidney Pie. Peter at Hyperlipid (high-fat-nutrition.blogspot.com) posted a recipe of sorts that was the inspiration for this version, but used beef steak. In this version, bison or venison or other wild game for the steak adds a nice Primal touch (certainly you may use beef if you prefer).

    Round steak is from the back hip end of the animal, and despite the "steak" in the cut name, it definitely needs s-l-o-w, moist braising to transform a tough, hard-worked cut into fork-tender stew meat. Those who dislike kidney can be kept happy with the steak and flavorful sauce.

SERVINGS: 3–5

INSTRUCTIONS:

Preheat oven to 325°F.

In a large skillet heat approx. half the fat over medium heat. Brown the steak meat and kidney pieces all over in small batches (so the meat doesn't steam). As each batch of meat is browned, remove it from the skillet to a casserole on the side. When all the meat has been browned (adding more fat as needed), deglaze the pan with ½ cup red wine, scraping up the brown bits from the bottom. Add the deglazing juices to the casserole.

Add 1 or 2 more tablespoons of fat to the skillet and heat on medium. Add the onion and garlic and sauté until the onion is translucent, about 3–5 minutes.

INGREDIENTS:

3 to 6 tablespoons high quality fat (lard, tallow, ghee, or butter)

1 to 2 pounds bison or venison round or sirloin, trimmed of gristle and cut into 1 inch dices

1 or 2 very fresh pig or lamb kidneys, about a ½ to ¾ pound, outer membrane and inner connective tissue core removed, cut into 1 inch dices

2 cup beef broth, red wine, or water, with more available if needed to add halfway through cooking

1 onion, finely chopped

2 or 3 cloves of garlic, finely chopped

1 carrot, cut into dice or rounds

1 can diced tomatoes or 2–3 fresh tomatoes, seeded and finely chopped

½ teaspoon sea salt

½ teaspoon freshly ground black pepper

3 to 6 inch segment of oxtail or the sirloin bones (*optional, but bones really enrich the stew*)

2 tablespoons crème fraîche or sour cream (*optional*)

Lower the heat if necessary to prevent the garlic and onions from burning.

Transfer the onions and garlic to the casserole along with the carrot and tomatoes, seasonings and the segment of oxtail, if using. Stir to combine.

Pour just enough broth, red wine, or water to cover over the ingredients in the casserole and stir gently to combine. Cover tightly with an ovenproof lid or aluminum foil and bake for at least 2 ½ hours or until steak and kidney pieces are fork-tender, perhaps as long as 3 hours. Check halfway through and add a bit of hot water if necessary to prevent drying out.

After removing casserole from the oven, if oxtail or bones were included, remove them and gristly pieces of connective tissue that didn't soften and melt. Adjust seasoning with salt and pepper if needed, then stir in crème fraîche or sour cream to thicken sauce *(optional)*. Garnish with chopped flat leaf Italian parsley. Serve with additional crème fraîche or sour cream at the table *(optional)*.

MILD LIVER PATÉ

The amazing Stephan Guyenet of WholeHealthSource.blogspot.com contributed this paté recipe, which might be more palatable for people reluctant to eat liver prepared more plainly. Stephan ranks chicken liver as the mildest liver in flavor, followed by pig liver, calf liver and beef liver (feel free to use whichever liver you prefer).

A small serving of liver from "clean" sources (preferably from producers of animals raised on their natural diets in low stress environments without antibiotics, hormones, or exposure to pesticides), once or twice a week, is excellent source of bioavailable iron, Vitamin A and Vitamin B12.

Paté may be eaten by itself or stuffed into celery sticks or hollowed cucumber "boats". Small dabs of paté placed on cucumber rounds, garnished with a few fish eggs, makes an elegant and easy appetizer.

INGREDIENTS:

1 pound calf liver, chicken liver or pig liver, chopped

½ onion, chopped finely
2 large carrots, chopped
½ stick of butter

1 4-inch sprig of rosemary, leaves removed from stem

3 sprigs of fresh thyme, leaves removed from stems

3 eggs

SERVINGS: 8–12

INSTRUCTIONS:

Sauté onions and carrots in one tablespoon butter until the onions are browned and the carrots are soft. Add the chopped liver, herbs and remaining butter and cook until the liver is cooked all the way through. Crack the eggs into the pan and stir until they're cooked. Add salt.

Put everything into a food processor or blender and purée until smooth. Serve with raw vegetable sticks.

CHOPPED LIVER

If your grandmother used to make chopped liver, this recipe is probably similar to hers. Similar, but likely not exactly the same, as every grandmother has her own specific methods and ingredient amounts that she believes create the perfect chopped liver. Traditional chopped liver recipes almost always contains onions and hard boiled eggs, and for good reason. Try this dish and you'll find out why.

INGREDIENTS:

3 to 6 tablespoons high quality fat (lard, tallow, ghee, or butter) or oil

1 onion, finely chopped

1 pound chicken livers, rinsed and patted dry

4 hard boiled eggs, finely chopped or grated

Salt and pepper to taste

SERVINGS: 8–12

INSTRUCTIONS:

Sauté the onion in several tablespoons of fat: butter, lard or oil. The onions should just be getting soft but nowhere near browned when you add the liver to the pan. Flip the livers once or twice until they are cooked through but still slightly pink in the center, about 10 minutes. Let onion and liver cool. Slice the livers into small pieces with a knife then transfer to a bowl and add chopped egg in small batches, mashing the mixture with a fork as you go. If the texture seems dry, add a little bit of oil. Some people prefer the end result to have some texture, others like it totally smooth. Mash until you reach your desired consistency.

MARROW AND PARSLEY SPREAD

Marrow is the soft, fatty filling in the hollow center of leg bones, a richly flavored treat considered by many to be a delicacy. Marrow bones can be purchased at most meat counters, although you might have to make a special request ahead of time. Briefly cooking the bones softens the fatty marrow and turns it into a runny, velvety consistency. It can be eaten straight from the bones with a tiny spoon, but we like to add a sprinkle of parsley salad on top to lighten and brighten the flavor.

INGREDIENTS:

2 beef or veal marrow bones
¼ cup finely chopped parsley
1 tablespoon finely chopped shallots
2 teaspoons olive oil
1 teaspoon squeeze of fresh lemon juice
¼ teaspoon lemon zest
Salt to taste

SERVINGS: 2–4

INSTRUCTIONS:

Preheat oven to 450°F. Put bones in a foil-lined baking dish. Cook until marrow is soft, about 15 minutes.

While marrow is cooking, combine parsley, shallot, olive oil, lemon juice and zest and salt in small bowl.

To serve, scoop out marrow and sprinkle with parsley salad.

GRILLED SWEETBREADS

Sweetbreads are prized by chefs for a silky, buttery texture and delicate flavor. Although not pretty to look at in raw form, sweetbreads are quite unthreatening when cooked. Grilling sweetbreads is an easy way to prepare them at home and creates a crispy outside that perfectly contrasts the soft, delicate middle.

Sweetbreads can be special ordered from most butchers or found in some ethnic markets. Plan to cook them within a day of purchase to insure they are as fresh as possible. Boiling the sweetbreads briefly in vinegar and water removes any blood and impurities, improving both the flavor and texture. It also partially cooks the sweetbreads so they need less time on the grill and will be nicely browned when the middle is cooked, not charred black.

INGREDIENTS:

1 ½ pounds sweetbreads
3 quarts water
½ cup apple cider vinegar
1 tablespoon salt
2 tablespoons oil

SERVINGS: 4–6

INSTRUCTIONS:

Rinse sweetbreads well, then transfer to a large pot with water, vinegar, and salt. Bring to a boil over high heat, then reduce heat and simmer gently 10 minutes. Drain sweetbreads in a colander, then transfer to a bowl of ice and cold water to cool.

Drain sweetbreads, then pat dry gently but thoroughly and separate into pieces about 2–3 inches in length. In a bowl, coat the sweetbreads with oil then thread onto skewers, Season lightly with salt and pepper. For more flavor, consider sprinkling with fresh herbs before grilling or adding a very light coating of mustard.

Grill sweetbreads over medium-high heat with the grill cover on until golden brown and cooked through the middle, about five minutes on each side.

FOWL

Chicken is a nice change of pace from red meat and pork. The key is to forget all the dry, bland chicken breasts of your past and rediscover how intensely flavorful fowl can be. Rather than viewing the mild flavor of chicken as a negative, remember that its mild flavor makes chicken the perfect meat to be paired with more assertive seasonings. Curries and other blends of spices, fresh herbs and loads of garlic can all turn chicken into a memorable meal.

Chicken isn't the only fowl out there, however. Turkey, duck and goose are birds that tend to be relegated to holidays only, but there is no reason you can't start enjoying them more regularly. Know that duck and goose are tougher and fattier, and can't always be substituted in recipes that call for chicken or turkey.

As with other types of meat, buy organic whenever possible. Poultry labeled as "free-range" implies (but doesn't always guarantee) the birds were given access to the outdoors during their life. It does, however, mean the meat is free of hormones and antibiotics.

Heritage breeds of fowl are being raised by more and more farmers who want to preserve breeds that have been absent from American kitchens for decades. Heritage breeds are more expensive to raise, as their growth and reproduction occurs on a natural schedule rather than one supplemented by hormones and antibiotics. This makes them more expensive to buy, but heritage breeds are worth considering for their more intense flavor and the humane and sustainable way in which they are raised.

COCONUT CURRY

You can't go wrong with the combination of spicy curry and faintly sweet coconut milk. The flavors in this dish are assertive, but not so much that they'll put off less adventurous or younger palates.

SERVINGS: 3–4

INSTRUCTIONS:

Heat oil in a large skillet or flameproof casserole, add chicken or duck pieces and cook over medium-high heat 8–10 minutes, turning once or twice to brown exterior.

Remove meat pieces from the pan to a large plate or platter. If using duck and excessive fat renders out, pour all but 2 tablespoons of the fat from the pan (strain it and save for other uses). Add mustard seeds, and cook about 1 minute, until they begin to pop.

Add onion to the pan and cook, scraping up the fond, the flavorful brown bits on the bottom of the pan, until soft and golden.

Stir in garlic, ginger root, green chili, and ground spices; cook about 2 minutes. Stir in vinegar, then return pieces of meat to the pan, turning to coat the pieces all over with the spicy mixture.

INGREDIENTS:

4 chicken or duck quarters, bone-in and skinned (rabbit may be substituted)

2 tablespoons coconut oil
1 teaspoon mustard seeds
1 medium onion, finely chopped
3 garlic cloves, crushed
1 2-inch piece of ginger root, grated (or 1 ½ tablespoons jarred, minced ginger root)
1 green chili, seeds removed, finely chopped *(optional)*

1 teaspoon ground cumin
1 tablespoon ground coriander
1 teaspoon ground turmeric

Cayenne pepper or hot pepper sauce to taste

1 tablespoon white wine vinegar
1 ¼ cup coconut milk

1 head cauliflower, cut into 2 inch florets

For garnish: chopped cilantro and toasted unsweetened shredded coconut

Pour coconut milk over all and bring to a slow boil. Cover, reduce heat to low and simmer about 40 minutes, or until meat is fork tender. Add the cauliflower florets in the last 10 minutes of cooking and simmer until tender.

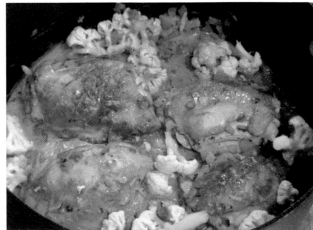

Easy, Slow-Cooked Chicken and Broth

This simple and lazy way to cook chicken results in extremely tender meat and flavorful broth. If you prepare a chicken weekly in this manner, you'll always have some homemade broth ready, plus a container of moist de-boned chicken in the refrigerator for quick meals and snacks. Be sure to use chicken on-the-bone for the most flavor and maximum mineral content in the meat and broth. True, you won't have that delicious crispy skin with this method, but this is so convenient and easy you might not even miss the crispy skin.

If you don't have a slow cooker you can use a stock pot on the range instead, but be sure to check periodically to see if minor temperature adjustments are necessary to maintain the water at a simmer. A chicken cooked in a pot on the range will cook faster, in about 2–3 hours. If you're short on time, consider using a pressure cooker instead. Use the same ingredients and add just enough water to cover the chicken. In less than an hour you'll have tender meat and a flavorful broth.

INGREDIENTS:

1 whole chicken, with neck and feet if available

1 onion, roughly chopped
1 leek, thinly sliced
2 celery ribs, finely chopped
1 or 2 carrots, finely chopped
1 bay leaf
6 whole peppercorns
2 to 4 whole garlic cloves

2 tablespoons of cider vinegar or the juice of ½ lemon

Additional chicken necks, backbones, and saved chicken bones from roast chicken *(optional)*

SERVINGS: Makes several quarts of broth depending on slow cooker capacity and 2–4 pounds of chicken, depending on chicken size.

INSTRUCTIONS:

Remove all packaging from chicken (check the cavity) and place in slow-cooker crock. Add the rest of the ingredients (except vinegar or lemon) around the chicken. Lightly salt and pepper.

Freezing Broth

Plastic containers made for freezing work well as they are flexible and can absorb expansion pressures. Wide-mouth quart glass canning jars will crack in the freezer, unless you leave ample room below the "jar shoulders" for expansion during freezing (always pre-chill in the refrigerator for best results with glass containers).

[Easy Slow-Cooked Chicken and Broth cont'd]

If you're using chicken feet, clean and then add to the pot. Feet make a really rich, gelatinous broth that is extra flavorful as well as soothing and nourishing for the lining of the GI tract— try sourcing from local poultry producers, local Asian markets, or online pastured chicken retailers.

Fill the slow cooker with water to about 2 inches from the top of the crock (do not overfill or liquid might bubble out). Add the vinegar or lemon juice to the water.

Set slow cooker temp to low and cook until meat is tender and at least 170°F, about 6 hours. Turn the chicken once during cooking for more even cooking. For faster cooking, set the slow cooker to high for about 3–4 hours, but keep in mind that slower cooked chicken is more tender. Don't be tempted to cook the chicken all day (like you can with chicken bones alone) as that will transfer too much of the chicken's flavor to the broth and create dry chicken meat.

Set a large platter or wide shallow bowl next to the slow cooker to receive the chicken. Carefully lift the chicken with a strong spatula or wooden spoon underneath or inside the cavity and tongs from above, letting it drain a moment over the pot. If really well cooked, the chicken meat may even come off the bones as it is lifted, in which case you can cut the chicken up or break it apart in the pot before transferring chicken pieces with tongs to the platter.

Let chicken set for a few minutes until it has cooled enough to handle. While still warm, remove the meat from the carcass, returning skin, bones, joints and cartilage to the broth. Serve the meat right away or store it in the refrigerator in an airtight container, ladling a cup of strained broth over the meat to keep it moist.

At this point the broth is usable, but the flavor and color is still on the weak side. After all the skin/bones, cartilage, and small bits of meat are back in the broth in the slow cooker, add water if needed. Continue to simmer broth and carcass for several more hours or as long as 24 hours. If simmered a very long time, the contents will begin to turn a rich golden brown and a deep chicken flavor will develop.

Turn off slow-cooker, let cool at least one hour, then ladle broth through a fine mesh strainer into storage containers. After chilling, the solid layer of fat that has collected at the top of the broth can be removed easily or left on top to "seal" the broth surface.

DUTCH OVEN CHICKEN

This recipe is adapted from a *Cook's Illustrated* technique, which was based on their experiments recreating a French-style chicken. The covered, slow-bake method using only the chicken's own juices creates a rich gelatinous chicken-y sauce and intense flavor in the meat that will wow your taste buds so much you might not even miss the crispy skin of a conventionally roasted chicken. Make this recipe with a truly free ranging heritage breed chicken like Poulet Rouge, and you might even swear you are dining in France.

INGREDIENTS:

1 whole roasting chicken (remove giblets from interior cavity)

1 teaspoon coarse sea salt
¼ teaspoon freshly ground black pepper

1 tablespoon fat (high quality non-hydrogenated lard, poultry fat, ghee, or olive oil)

½ cup finely chopped onion
¼ cup finely chopped celery
4–6 cloves of garlic, peeled
1 bay leaf

SERVINGS: 3–4

INSTRUCTIONS:

Place rack in lowest position of oven (remove top rack if there isn't enough clearance for the Dutch oven pot). Preheat oven to 250°F.

Dry chicken with paper towels to remove excess moisture from packaging. Season all over with salt and pepper.

Heat fat in Dutch oven on the stove over medium heat. When fat is hot and nearly smoking, place chicken breast side down in the hot pot. While chicken is browning, prepare vegetables, adding to the pan as you chop. Cook about 6–8 minutes total, until breast skin browns.

Turn chicken breast side up (a sturdy wooden spoon inserted into cavity is useful) and cook about 8 more minutes. Continue adding vegetables if you aren't yet finished prepping them.

Turn off heat. Cover pot with tight fitting lid (use a sheet of aluminum foil under the lid, too, if the lid doesn't create a good seal).

Place pot into oven and bake about 1 ½ hours for a small chicken (under 4 pounds) or about 2 hours for larger chickens (over 4 ½ pounds). Chicken is finished cooking when instant read thermometer shows a temperature of 175°F in the thigh meat not near a bone (thigh will wiggle freely in socket, too, and juices will run clear).

Transfer chicken to warm platter or grooved cutting board (some juices may escape) and cover loosely with the sheet of aluminum foil used to seal lid to pan. Let sit 20 minutes.

Strain juices from pot through a fine wire mesh strainer (save cooked vegetables for making broth with leftover chicken bones—see below) and let the fat rise to the top. Skim fat off and adjust seasoning to taste, salt and pepper if necessary. Keep juices warm until time to serve.

Carve chicken into quarters and serve with warm juices.

Place strained cooked vegetables, bones, skin, cartilage and leftover juices back in Dutch oven or in a slow cooker. Cover bones with cold filtered water

and 2 tablespoons of apple cider vinegar and let sit one hour. Then simmer over low temperature for at least 6–8 hours, up to 24 hours if using a slow cooker. Strain broth through fine wire mesh strainer to remove solids. Broth will keep in refrigerator for up to a week (reheat to a boil before consuming) or several months in the freezer (be sure to leave room at top of the container for expansion).

CHICKEN SOUP WITH COCONUT MILK

This basic soup template has infinite variation possibilities using leftover cooked chicken or turkey (or rabbit!) for a fast, satisfying soup entrée. Try fresh pea pods, strips of red pepper, steamed winter squash chunks, or even those small remainders of the week's leftovers that aren't enough for one serving. The curry powder, hot sauce, or red pepper flakes may be omitted or adjusted from mild to scorching.

INGREDIENTS:

1 can coconut milk

3 cups chicken stock (see recipe on page 72)

Juice of 1 lemon or 2 limes

2 teaspoons fresh ginger, peeled and grated or minced

3 inch section of lemongrass *(optional)*
1–2 carrots, thinly sliced

⅛–½ teaspoon Thai curry paste, or dash of hot sauce or ½ teaspoon crushed red pepper flakes

1 head of cauliflower, cut into small florets

1–2 cups cooked chicken meat, diced or uncooked chicken meat, cut into small strips

4 fresh basil leaves, chopped or 1 teaspoon dried basil

SERVINGS: 4

INSTRUCTIONS:

Place coconut milk, chicken stock, lemon or lime juice, ginger, lemongrass (if using), carrot, and Thai curry paste or other hot seasoning into a 2–4 quart sauce pan and bring to a simmer over medium-high heat. When carrots are about halfway cooked, add cauliflower florets and lower heat to medium, until the vegetables are all nearly cooked through, about 5–8 minutes. Add chicken meat and simmer a few more minutes (until chicken is cooked through if using raw chicken). Stir in chopped basil leaves and season with salt and more hot spice to taste. Remove lemongrass stalks, and serve in a bowl garnished with thinly sliced fresh basil leaves.

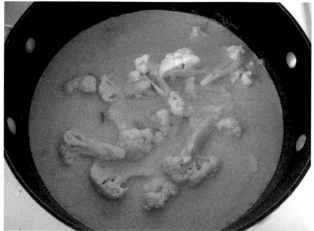

PEACHY CHICKEN SALAD

Poultry, fruit, and spices are mixed together, co-mingling into a blend of the familiar and the exotic. The addition of almonds and celery give the dish a nice crunch. This is a perfect summer salad for lunch or a picnic.

INGREDIENTS:

1 large ripe peach or nectarine, washed, pitted and chopped (no need to peel)

1 ½ cups diced cooked chicken breast
½ cup finely diced celery
A handful of almonds, chopped

Dressing:
3 tablespoons homemade mayonnaise (see recipe on page 224)

½ teaspoon unfiltered apple cider vinegar (preferably raw)

2 tablespoons orange juice, freshly squeezed

2 tablespoons fresh parsley, chopped (or 2 teaspoons dried)

¼ to ½ teaspoon curry powder
⅛ teaspoon ground cloves

Garnish: whole leaves of fresh butter lettuce

SERVINGS: 2

INSTRUCTIONS:

Toss the peaches, chicken, celery and almonds together.

Whisk together the dressing ingredients and pour over the chicken mixture. Toss gently to coat. Serve right away on leaves of butter lettuce, or chill in the fridge before serving.

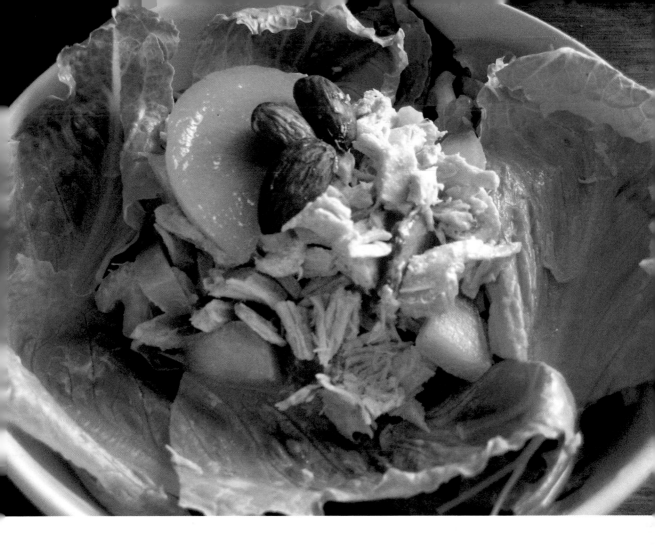

Chicken and Fennel Stew

Chicken thighs are more tender and flavorful than other cuts and make this stew extra rich, although drumsticks could easily be substituted. The combination of both fennel bulb and fennel seeds give a very subtle but intriguing flavor to the stew. Fennel seeds can be found in the spice aisle of most grocery stores and have a complex flavor with a delicate hint of licorice.

INGREDIENTS:

2 pounds chicken thighs (about 8 small thighs)

½ onion, finely chopped
1 small fennel bulb, thinly sliced
½ pound of mushrooms, sliced
2 garlic cloves, finely chopped

1 teaspoon fennel seeds, finely chopped until powdery

½ teaspoon saffron threads
2 cups Belgian beer or chicken broth
½ cup heavy cream or coconut milk
1 small bunch kale, finely chopped
½ cup finely chopped parsley

SERVINGS: 4–6

INSTRUCTIONS:

In a deep ovenproof pan, brown chicken over medium-high heat with a little bit of oil, about 4–6 minutes a side. Remove thighs from pan. Add onion, fennel and mushrooms and sauté until soft, about 5 minutes. If there isn't enough fat from the chicken, add some oil or butter to the pan.

In a small bowl combine a tablespoon of beer or broth with the saffron, and break and mash the threads with the back of the spoon so the saffron threads bleed out some color. Add this mixture plus the rest of the beer or broth to the pot, followed by the garlic and fennel seeds. Bring to a gentle boil for several minutes. Return chicken to pot. Put on lid and simmer about 25 minutes, until chicken is done. Remove from heat and stir in cream or coconut milk and kale. Garnish with chopped parsley.

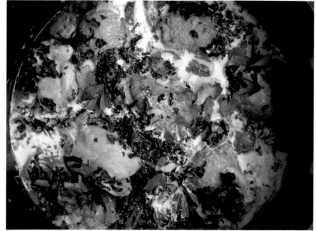

MOROCCAN CHICKEN

Moroccan stews like this one, made with either meat or poultry, aromatic spices and vegetables, are called *tagines*. Don't be turned off by the long list of ingredients; they're mostly spices that are all easily found at the grocery store. This particular combination of spices makes a fairly spicy stew. If you don't want it too hot, hold back a little on the turmeric, cayenne and paprika and use more cinnamon and cumin.

INGREDIENTS:

2 tablespoons oil
1 onion, finely diced
3 garlic cloves, finely diced
1 tablespoon finely chopped ginger
½ teaspoon turmeric
½ teaspoon cinnamon
1 ½ teaspoons paprika
½ teaspoon coriander
½ teaspoon cumin
¼ teaspoon cayenne *(optional)*
4 chicken thighs
1 14.5-ounce can diced tomatoes in juice
2 cups water
½ cup finely chopped cilantro
1 lemon, thinly sliced
2 cups green beans, cut in half
¼ cup finely chopped mint
Juice from 1 lemon

SERVINGS: 4

INSTRUCTIONS:

Sauté onion, garlic and ginger in oil until soft and slightly browned. Add spices and sauté a minute more. Then add chicken, tomatoes, water, cilantro and sliced lemon. Simmer with a lid for 30 minutes. Add green beans, mint and lemon juice. Simmer a few more minutes until green beans are done. Serve over cauliflower rice (**see recipe on page 184**).

Roasted Turkey Breast with Herb Butter

It's a shame that turkey is usually relegated to Thanksgiving. This is partly because of tradition, and partly because roasting a whole turkey seems like too much work for a regular night of a week. If you buy just the bone-in turkey breasts, however, rather than a whole turkey, the task is less daunting.

A generous drizzle of butter keeps the meat moist and creates crispy, deeply browned skin. As we all know, one of the best things about turkey is leftovers. Roast the turkey early in the week and you'll have enough meat for several lunches.

INGREDIENTS:

4–5 pound bone-in turkey breast
3 tablespoons unsalted butter
1 tablespoon finely chopped fresh sage
1 tablespoon fresh or 1 teaspoon dried thyme
¼ cup finely chopped fresh parsley
¼ teaspoon pepper
1 teaspoon salt
1 garlic clove, finely chopped
1 cup chicken or turkey broth

SERVINGS: 6

INSTRUCTIONS:

Preheat oven to 425°F.

Gently melt the butter with the herbs, salt and pepper. Remove from heat and add the garlic. Gently pull the skin away from the turkey meat and drizzle a little bit of butter under the skin. Drizzle or brush the rest of the butter over the top of the turkey.

Roast the turkey uncovered in a roasting pan for 45 minutes. Then, add the broth to the pan and continue to roast until the temperature of the turkey reaches 165–170, about another 45 minutes. If the skin on the top of the turkey begins to get too dark, lightly cover it with foil.

Remove the turkey from the oven and pour any liquid into a sauté pan. Simmer the liquid on the stove for several minutes to reduce the liquid slightly. Slice the turkey off the bone, drizzle turkey juices on top. Serve warm or at room temperature.

TURKEY KEBABS

These kebabs are a little different than your typical skewer lined with cubes of meat and vegetables. Instead, ground turkey is formed into an elongated meatball and grilled. The addition of spices makes the meat incredibly flavorful and slightly spicy. These kebabs could be served either as a main course or appetizer.

INGREDIENTS:

1 ½ pounds turkey breast, de-boned, trimmed of most of the skin and cut into thin strips

1 garlic clove
1 tablespoon olive oil
1 egg
½ teaspoon cumin
½ teaspoon paprika
½ teaspoon salt
¼ teaspoon cinnamon
¼ teaspoon or less cayenne pepper
2 tablespoons cup finely chopped parsley
1 tablespoon finely chopped mint

SERVINGS: 6–8 kebabs

INSTRUCTIONS:

In a food processor, blend meat until ground. Add all remaining ingredients and pulse a few times until well blended. Lightly grease your hands then form meat into meatballs that are longer and more oval in shape than regular meatballs. Drizzle the formed meatballs with oil and slide a skewer through them. Gently lift onto a hot grill and grill for 6–8 minutes a side.

BRAISED DUCK WITH BOK CHOY

A whole duck can be challenging to cook, since each part of the duck cooks differently. To become tender, the thigh meat is best when roasted, but the breasts are best seared so the thick, fatty skin becomes crispy. This recipe provides different cooking methods for each and the result is a succulent, rich meal. The addition of bok choy adds both color and a lighter flavor.

INGREDIENTS:

1 5–7 pound duck
1 carrot, roughly chopped
1 stick of celery, roughly chopped
1 large white or yellow onion, roughly chopped
1 tablespoon ginger root, finely chopped
2 garlic cloves, finely chopped
1 teaspoon grated lime zest
1 tablespoon wheat-free tamari
6 bok choy
2 tablespoons oil for searing

SERVINGS: 4

INSTRUCTIONS:

Remove excess fat and neck from inside body cavity, saving the neck for stock. Cut off legs, wings, and breasts from duck, or ask your butcher to do it for you, making sure to save the carcass for the stock. Cut off the flap of fat that remains on the carcass and also remove any fat that seems excessive from the duck pieces. Save all the fat, as it can be rendered later and the fat can be used for other recipes.

Break the carcass up into smaller pieces and put it in a large soup pot with the carrot, celery, half of the chopped onion and 1 quart of water. The water should almost completely cover the carcass. Add a dash of salt and pepper and bring to a boil. Then reduce heat so the broth continues to gently simmer uncovered for 1 hour, skimming off foam if it gathers on the top. After an hour, strain the stock through a colander or fine mesh sieve and discard solids. Skim excess fat off the top of the stock. You won't have much more than 2 cups of stock remaining.

When stock is completed, preheat oven to 350°F.

Pat legs and wings dry and season with a dash of salt and pepper.

Heat 1 tablespoon oil in a large, deep ovenproof pot. Add legs and wings and brown each side, about 8 minutes total cooking time. Remove from pot and set aside. Lower heat and add ginger, garlic, lime zest and remaining onion and sauté several minutes until onion is translucent. Add tamari, duck stock, legs and wings. Bring to a boil then cover the pot and put in the oven for 1 hour. After cooking, remove meat from pot and place in serving dish (left on the bone, or cut off). Save the broth.

Next, pat duck breasts dry and lightly salt. Over high heat, warm 1 tablespoon oil then add duck breasts, skin side down, and cook until skin is golden and as crisp as possible, 4–8 minutes. Pour oil out of pan and flip breasts skin side up. Cook 10–12 minutes more to desired doneness. Or, if the oven is still on you can put the pan in the oven after searing and roast the breasts uncovered to desired doneness. Duck breast is typically served fairly pink and medium rare, which registers around 135 on a thermometer. Add the duck to the serving dish, either whole or sliced.

To finish the dish, bring the broth to a simmer. Add bok choy and simmer

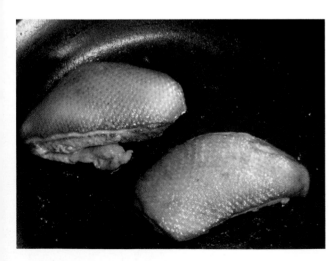
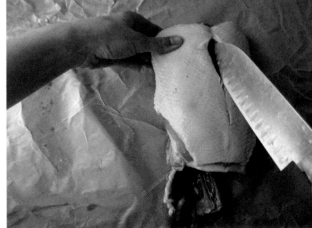

with a lid for 4–6 minutes, lifting the lid once to rearrange bok choy so the ones on the top come in contact with the broth.

Arrange bok choy on the serving platter with meat. Drizzle the broth over the top if desired.

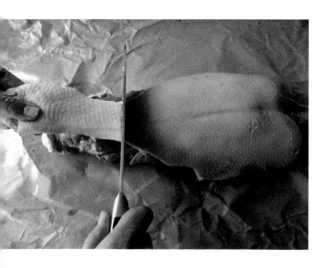

How to Cut a Whole Duck

If you ask, your butcher might cut up the duck for you, but with a little practice you'll become quite good at it yourself.

As you cut, use your fingers to feel where joints connect; this will help determine where to cut when removing the wings and thighs. The combination of a sharp, thin knife and kitchen scissors works well for this job. The scissors can be used to trim the skin away from the meat and cut through tendons.

1. Lay the duck on its breast and feel where the wing joint attaches to the body. The joint should come off with the wing. This can be easier if you first pull the wing away from the body, snapping the joint so it pops loose. As you cut the wing off, be careful not to cut into the breast meat.

2. Turn the duck on its back and pull one thigh away from the body. Cut slowly through the skin between the thigh and the breast. When you reach the joint, pull on the thigh to snap it out of joint and then keep cutting, following the contours of the backbone. Detach the thigh. Repeat to cut off the other thigh. After removing the thighs, the only meat that should remain on the carcass is the breasts.

3. With the tip of your knife, make a shallow cut running along one side of the breastplate, which is right in the middle of the two breasts. Slowly continue to cut, pulling the breast meat away from the body as you separate the meat from the carcass.

SEAFOOD

From flakey to buttery, and from slick and smooth to rich and meaty, seafood offers an astonishing array of textures that respond well to almost any method of cooking. Grilling, pan frying, baking and poaching are all suitable. As far as seasoning goes, seafood doesn't demand much. Most types of fish and shellfish are perfectly happy with simple lemon and butter. But why not have a little fun and try something new? The mild flavor of most seafood makes it the perfect protein to pair with richly flavored broths and an array of fresh herbs and spices with a little bit of kick. Surrounding seafood with enticing flavors can coax even those who claim not to eat it much to take a bite.

Fish is a rich source of omega-3 fatty acids and a whole spectrum of vitamins and minerals. Studies have shown that the benefits of eating seafood in moderation outweigh the risks of ingesting toxins from polluted waters. However, serving seafood these days comes with a certain amount of responsibility. Is the fish you're serving farm raised or caught in the wild? Has it been fished in a way that does not threaten the environment and other species? Has it been exposed to toxins that you should avoid consuming regularly, if ever? Bringing home a simple fillet for dinner can be overwhelming until you commit to one simple thing: buy from a trusted source. Talk to the people you're buying your seafood from, ask questions and if you don't trust their answers, find a new place to shop. A little self-education also goes a long way. The list of the most sustainable and least contaminated seafood choices is always changing, but up-to-date information is available online on sites like The Monterey Bay Aquarium (www.montereybayaquarium.org) and the Environmental Defense Fund (www.edf.org).

SALMON CHOWDER

This hearty nod to New England clam chowder retains the creamy, almost stew-like character of the classic, yet contains no milk or excessive starch. This makes good use of thrifty wild-caught canned salmon that is available year round and easy to stock in the pantry, but it's also excellent made with leftover cooked wild-caught salmon fillet. Either way, your omega-3 fatty acids are covered with both forms of wild-caught salmon.

For added interest and a wider variety of seafood nutrients, use one 4 ounce can of salmon, but add chopped clams and smoked mussels, including the juices.

SERVINGS: 4

INSTRUCTIONS:

Cook the bacon in a large saucepan over medium-low heat, until the bacon fat is released. Add onion, dill, bay leaf, black pepper, and cayenne and cook until the bacon is barely crispy.

Add the celery, turnips or cauliflower and chicken broth and simmer until the vegetables are almost tender, about 5–7 minutes. Add salmon chunks and the juices and simmer a few more minutes to heat through.

Stir in the coconut milk. Bring to a slow boil, then simmer over low heat for a few minutes. Remove bay leaf.

INGREDIENTS:

3 slices of bacon or 3 ounces of pancetta, diced

1 small onion, finely chopped

1 teaspoon dried dill or 1 tablespoon chopped fresh dill (optional)

1 bay leaf
Black pepper, to taste

1/8 teaspoon cayenne pepper, or to taste (optional)

2 stalks celery, finely chopped

1 1/2 to 2 cups finely chopped peeled turnips or small cauliflower florets

1 1/2 cups chicken broth (see recipe on page 72)

1 7.5-ounce can red salmon, separated into chunks, reserve juices for soup

1 14-ounce can full fat coconut milk
Extra minced dill for garnish

[Salmon Chowder cont'd]

Serve soup very warm in pre-warmed bowls, garnished with dill.

FISH BROTH

Traditionally, fish broth is made with heads and carcasses of non-oily fish, but these days those parts can be difficult to source unless you have a good fishmonger, do your own fishing, or know someone who fishes. Even without the fish trimmings, you can make a nourishing and quickly improvised fish broth by using bonito flakes.

Bonito flakes are shaved dried fish usually stocked in the "International aisle" of supermarkets or in Japanese or Asian-style supermarkets. Once opened, bonito flakes need to be stored in the refrigerator in an airtight container and used relatively quickly. Smaller packets of bonito flakes may be found in Asian supermarkets or from online retailers, as an alternative to buying larger bags that might not be used fast enough. Miso broth can be used in place of fish broth if bonito flakes prove too difficult to find.

INGREDIENTS:

1 cup bonito flakes
2 quarts cold water

¼ cup rice wine vinegar
(or cider vinegar)

SERVINGS: 6–8

INSTRUCTIONS:

Place all ingredients in a large saucepan and bring to a boil over medium-high heat. Lower heat and simmer for 2–3 hours. Skim surface periodically if foam develops.

Let liquid cool and strain with a fine mesh strainer. Store broth in airtight containers in the refrigerator (up to one week) or freeze (be sure to cool first and allow adequate room in container for expansion).

Fish Soup with Coconut Milk

This is a delicious, fast way to increase intake of healthy omega-3 fatty acids from oily cold water fish. Adding steamed cauliflower florets gives it the consistency of a chowder, but without the starch of traditional chowders that use potatoes. Finely chopped, steamed turnips may also be used.

INGREDIENTS:

1 can coconut milk, about 14 ounces (NOT "light" or reduced fat)

3 cups chicken stock (see recipe on page 72) or fish stock (see recipe on page 100)

1 pound fresh fish, skin removed, cut into 1 inch dices (any kind or combination, but preferably a cold water, oily fish variety)

Juice of 1 lemon or 2 limes

2 teaspoons fresh ginger, peeled and grated or minced

1 or 2 carrots, sliced into thin "coins" or fine julienne strips

3 inch section of lemongrass *(optional)*

1 head of cauliflower, separated into small florets and steamed *(optional)*

4 fresh basil leaves, chopped, plus extra leaves cut into thin slices for garnish

Thai red curry paste (½ teaspoon or more)

Dash of Tabasco or other brand hot pepper sauce, or to taste (may also use red pepper flakes)

Sea salt and freshly ground black pepper, to taste

½ pound peeled shrimp *(optional)*

SERVINGS: 4

INSTRUCTIONS:

Place coconut milk, stock, fish, lemon or lime juice, ginger, carrots and lemongrass and cauliflower (if using), into a 2–4 quart sauce pan and bring to a simmer over medium-high heat, then reduce heat until gently simmering. Stir in chopped basil leaves and season with red curry paste and sea salt, to taste. Soup is ready when fish is cooked through, about 10–15 minutes. If adding shrimp, put them in the broth after simmering for ten minutes and cook another 5–6 minutes. Remove lemongrass and serve hot, garnished with thinly sliced basil in each bowl.

STUFFED MACKEREL

This is a deliciously simple and versatile recipe taking advantage of a fish loaded with healthy omega-3 oil. If you can't find mackerel at the store, substitute any white-fleshed fish, such as whole trout. You can also use fillets instead of a whole fish, and simply pile the stuffing around the pieces of fish.

INGREDIENTS:

1 or 2 whole cleaned mackerel
1 large shallot, finely chopped
1–2 cups chopped mushrooms
4 large sage leaves, finely chopped
1–2 tablespoons oil

Oven-safe parchment paper or aluminum foil

SERVINGS: Varies, depending on size of fish. Stuffing can easily be multiplied to make more.

INSTRUCTIONS:

Preheat the oven to 350°F.

Place the fish on a generously sized piece of parchment paper (enough to wrap up fish completely).

Combine shallots, mushrooms and sage and sauté briefly in oil to soften mushrooms. Stuff as much of the stuffing mixture as you can into the fish's internal cavity and place the rest underneath and on top of the fish. Fold the parchment paper over the mackerel to enclose completely.

Bake for 30–40 minutes or until done. When cooked, the flesh near the spine should appear opaque and flaky, rather than translucent.

NIÇOISE SALAD

This salad is so tasty and satisfying you should consider eating it any time of day (yes, even for breakfast). We've revamped the classic Niçoise Salad with this quick-to-assemble colorful *Primal Blueprint* version, using convenient pantry and refrigerator staple items as well as some specialty ingredients that add nourishing bonuses.

Don't save beautiful fish eggs just for fancy occasions; bright orange salmon eggs add an easy eye-catching garnish to everyday savory dishes, and like all eggs, pack a powerful punch of nutrition into a tiny package. Salmon, carp, and tobiko fish roe are often available for just a few dollars in the gourmet coolers of well-stocked supermarkets. Unopened jars keep for a long time in the refrigerator; once opened, use within a week.

INGREDIENTS:

2 cups tender lettuce greens or watercress, torn into bite sized pieces

½ can tuna, packed in olive oil, flaked but not drained

1 tablespoon raw apple cider vinegar
1 teaspoon rustic grainy mustard
½ ripe avocado, diced

1 hard boiled egg, cut into wedges or slices

1 lacto-fermented cucumber pickle, sliced

1 tablespoon salmon eggs (roe), or other salt-cured fish egg variety

SERVINGS: 1 light meal or 2 side salads

INSTRUCTIONS:

Place washed and torn lettuce greens in a shallow bowl or on a plate. Top with flaked tuna, drizzling the olive oil from the tuna over the lettuce greens. Mix the mustard with the cider vinegar in a small bowl, then drizzle over salad. Toss lightly to blend oil and mustard-vinegar mixture.

Scatter remaining ingredients except salmon roe on top of tuna and salad greens. Garnish with salmon roe in center of salad.

The Mother of All Vinegars

Raw unfiltered cider vinegar (with the "mother"—a cobweb-like substance that develops during fermentation and rests at the bottom of the bottle) is great for digestion, as is the old-fashioned cucumber pickle (traditionally preserved with lacto-fermentation instead of modern industrial pickling techniques). Look for probiotic-rich pickles in the refrigerated case with "raw" foods at your local health food store, though sometimes you can still find these at well-stocked conventional supermarkets with the other chilled pickles.

[Niçoise Salad cont'd]

Additional suggestions:

The classic Niçoise Salad also includes lightly steamed slender green beans (haricots verts), and tender chunks of cooked new potatoes (warm or chilled).

FISH PATTY CAKES

Fish cakes are extremely popular in families with young children, as it's an easy meal to make that nearly everyone enjoys. Additionally, canned fish is an economical way to enjoy nutritious wild-caught fish year-round. Most fish cake recipes use breadcrumbs, but we'll use gluten-free coconut flour instead. Also, sardines can be used, but expect a fishier flavor.

If the fish comes with skins and bones don't remove them. Simply mash them up as they are soft and edible and will disappear, providing absorbable minerals and trace nutrients (you might want to be alone in the kitchen at this stage if you think family members will object).

SERVINGS: 3–4

INSTRUCTIONS:

Place drained fish in a large bowl and flake with a fork. Add eggs, onions, herbs, mustard, salt and black pepper and stir to mix well. Add coconut flour a little at a time, mixing well and stopping when the mixture will hold together in a patty shape.

Heat a wide skillet with some fat over medium heat.

Shape mixture into 3 inch patties (don't make them larger or they will be too hard to turn over in one piece).

INGREDIENTS:

2 cans of wild-caught salmon or mackerel (or 1 can of each), about 14–15 ounces each, drained and flaked

2 eggs, beaten

¼ cup finely minced onion or scallions, raw or lightly cooked

2 tablespoons chopped parsley or dill (2 teaspoons if dried)

1 teaspoon prepared mustard
½ teaspoon sea salt

½ teaspoon freshly ground black pepper

Approximately ¼ cup coconut flour, more if the mixture is too wet to hold together, less if the mixture is too dry

High quality cooking fat, such as ghee or non-hydrogenated lard (don't use plain butter or extra virgin olive oil as it will brown too much)

[Fish Patty Cakes cont'd]

Keep the patties the same diameter and thickness for even cooking.

Place patties into hot pan (do not crowd them) and cook until golden and lightly browned, about 5–7 minutes. Try not to disturb or turn prematurely for the best outer crust formation. Using a flexible thin pancake turner/spatula, flip over fish cakes, being careful to not break them. Cook the other side.

If cooking fish cakes in more than one batch to avoid crowding, keep cooked fish cakes warm on an oven-safe dish or plate in a 225°F oven.

Serve with Lemon Caper Sauce **(see recipe on page 232).**

Canned vs. Fresh Salmon

Farmed salmon doesn't can well, which means the majority of canned salmon is wild. Although fresh wild caught salmon is preferred (it contains more good fats than most canned salmon), salmon sold in cans is an affordable substitute.

TARAMASALATA
(GREEK FISH ROE SPREAD)

Grok, our prototypical hunter-gatherer ancestor, loved nutrient-dense eggs of all sorts, including fish eggs, sometimes called roe. Taramasalata is a classic tangy Greek fish roe spread or dip that is great paired with sliced radishes, celery sticks, carrot sticks, olives, and nut-meal crackers. The traditional recipes often use starchy stale bread and mashed potato as extenders, but this Grok-approved version substitutes finely chopped blanched almonds instead.

Of course, the right oil is important too, so instead of the soybean oil often used in commercially prepared taramasalata, we'll use a healthier nut oil or olive oil. (Be aware that extra virgin olive oil creates a much more assertive flavor than mild olive oil or most nut oils.)

INGREDIENTS:

½ cup blanched almonds*
1 garlic clove

2 ounces (about ¼ cup) fish roe (cod or carp)

2 scallions or small bunch of chives, finely sliced (divided use)

Juice of 1 lemon
⅓ cup light olive oil or a nut oil
Sea salt, to taste

SERVINGS: About 1 cup

INSTRUCTIONS:

In a food processor, pulse the almonds and garlic until they are the texture of fine crumbs (avoid processing too much or you will have paste). Add one half of the scallions, the roe, and the lemon juice, pulse again. Drizzle in the oil slowly while the food processor runs until the mixture is creamy and emulsified. Add a bit more oil if too thick.

Adjust flavor with salt if needed.

Roe, Roe, Roe Your Boat

Fish roe, either carp or cod, is available in jars or cans at Greek, Middle Eastern, or Asian food markets. In jars the roe may be labeled as tarama, and in cans it may be labeled as pressed fish roe and will need to be broken up with a fork after opening. Jarred tarama is salted and will keep for about a year if kept unopened and well chilled in the refrigerator or freezer, so it is very handy for making taramasalata as well as garnishing or whisking into scrambled eggs, soups, or salad dressings. Larger jars of carp and cod roe are not nearly as pricey as tiny jars of fancy grade caviar and roe found in specialty gourmet sections of grocery stores.

[Taramasalata cont'd]

Serve in a small dish garnished with remaining scallions on top, drizzled with a bit of extra virgin olive oil, with sliced vegetables or olives for scooping.

Store tightly covered and well chilled in the refrigerator. Use within 5 days.

*To blanch whole almonds, pour boiling water over a bowl of whole almonds to cover, let sit 1 minute. Then drain, rinse with cold water, and drain again. Pat almonds dry and "pinch" each almond to slip skin off. Do not let almonds soak too long or they will lose crispness.

WHOLE FISH BAKED IN SEA SALT

A whole fish is impressive on the table and cooking it encased in a hard shell of salt ensures that the meat will stay moist and flavorful. Don't be alarmed by all the salt in the recipe—it seals in the moisture without penetrating the skin and over-seasoning the fish. The Italians perfected this method of cooking and you can continue to hone the recipe to your liking. If you don't care for the delicate licorice flavor of fennel seeds, use another spice or simply stuff the fish with fresh herbs.

SERVINGS:
2–3 pound fish yields 2–3 servings
4–5 pound fish yields 3–6 servings

INSTRUCTIONS:

Preheat oven to 450°F.

Line a baking pan with foil and let foil hang over the edge.

Rinse fish and pat dry. Sprinkle fennel and pepper inside the fish and stuff with lemon slices and parsley.

INGREDIENTS:

1 2–5 pound whole striped bass or other fish, cleaned, gutted, and scaled

½ teaspoon fennel seeds, crushed and chopped with a knife

¼ teaspoon black pepper
A half-dozen parsley sprigs
3–4 thin slices of lemon
2 egg whites
4 cups coarse kosher salt

Serve with lemon wedges

Whisk egg whites by hand or in a mixer. First the eggs will become foamy—continue whisking until the consistency is stiffer and you can pull up peaks with the whisk. Gently stir in salt.

Spread about 1 cup of the salt mixture in the bottom of pan, spreading it out to the length of the fish. Set the fish on top. Cover the fish with the remaining salt, packing it down gently but firmly with your hands. The entire fish should be covered with the salt.

Bake 25 minutes. Remove from oven and let sit 10 minutes. Rap on crust with a knife or spoon to crack it open. Use your hands to carefully remove chunks of salt from the top of the fish and gently brush off the remaining salt with your fingers or a towel. Remove lemon and parsley from cavity. The flesh directly next to the opening of the cavity may be overly salty, but the rest of the fish should be perfectly seasoned.

To serve, peel back skin and remove top fillet. Pull out bones, then remove second fillet.

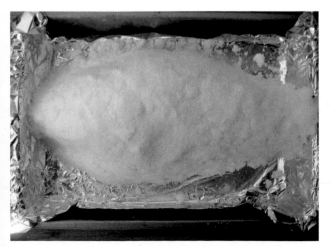
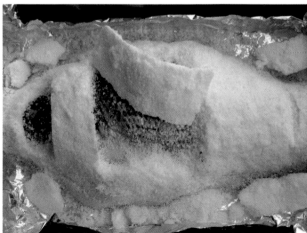

Shrimp Cakes with Spinach Slaw and Coconut Almond Dressing

These shrimp cakes flavored with coconut milk and cilantro are elegant enough to serve as the main course at a dinner party and easy enough to whip up as an afternoon snack. You can make larger shrimp cakes, but bite-sized is perfect for finger food or as a garnish over salad.

For the slaw, crunchy cabbage and carrots combined with spinach are just the right combination, especially when dressed with an exotically flavored dressing. The slight sweetness of coconut milk and rich almond butter in the dressing are balanced with a squirt of lime and the bright, clean flavors of mint and cilantro.

INGREDIENTS:

Shrimp Cakes:

1 pound raw shrimp, shelled, deveined and roughly chopped

¼ cup coconut milk

2 tablespoons chopped cilantro

1 teaspoon minced jalapeño or Thai pepper

Salad:

4 ounces fresh spinach leaves (about 2 large handfuls)

1 cup grated purple cabbage

2 carrots, grated

1 cucumber, finely chopped

Coconut Almond Dressing: (see recipe on page 222)

SERVINGS: 3–4

INSTRUCTIONS:

In a food processor pulse shrimp, coconut milk, cilantro and hot pepper 10–15 times until ingredients are combined but the texture is still slightly chunky. Heat several tablespoons of oil in a pan over medium heat. For bite-sized shrimp cakes, use a tablespoon measurement to scoop up shrimp batter and drop it into the pan. This will make 16–18 small cakes. Cook each side 2–3 minutes, until nicely browned. Set shrimp cakes aside.

Mix the salad ingredients together in a bowl and toss with Coconut Almond dressing. Garnish with shrimp cakes on top.

Chopped Yellowfin Tuna Salad with Avocado and Bacon

This colorful salad has a satisfying array of textures from crispy bacon, fatty tuna and creamy avocado. These ingredients lend an incredible amount of richness to the salad, whereas flavors of fresh dill, lemon and chopped red onion add a light and refreshing kick. Together, the ingredients have so much flavor that you don't even need dressing—a squirt of lemon will do.

INGREDIENTS:

¾ to 1 pound yellowfin tuna steak
¼ cup finely chopped red onion

1 avocado, peeled, pitted and cut into small pieces

2 tablespoons finely chopped fresh dill or other herb

½ cup crumbled cooked bacon
2 tablespoons lemon juice
Oil for searing

SERVINGS: 3–4

INSTRUCTIONS:

Heat heavy skillet over high heat 2 minutes. Brush tuna with oil and sprinkle lightly with salt and pepper. Place in the hot skillet and sear until browned on the outside, about 3 minutes per side for medium-rare, less for rare. Cool tuna; dice finely. Mix with other ingredients. Serve alone or over mixed greens.

PAN FRIED OYSTERS WITH DIPPING SAUCE

Nothing brings you closer to the feeling of standing next to the ocean than the taste of fresh oysters. If you're not up for raw oysters, then fried oysters are the next best thing. Coconut flour gives the oysters a crispy coating and a dipping sauce adds extra flavor.

INGREDIENTS:

6 oysters in the shell
½ cup coconut flour
1 egg
¼ teaspoon black pepper
¼ teaspoon salt
¼–½ cup oil for frying

Dipping Sauce (can easily be doubled for more oysters):
¼ cup mayonnaise (see recipe on page 224)

1 tablespoon lemon juice
2 teaspoons finely chopped red onion
1 tablespoon finely chopped dill
Dash of hot sauce *(optional)*

SERVINGS: 1–2

INSTRUCTIONS:

To remove the oysters from the shell: Scrub oysters thoroughly under cold running water. Take an oyster knife in one hand and thick towel or glove in the other. With the towel, grip the shell in palm of your hand. Insert the tip of the oyster knife between shell halves at the narrow end of the oyster where the shell is "hinged" together. Gently twist the knife and apply pressure to pry the shell open. Run the knife along the length of the shell to open it entirely. Cut the oyster out of the shell.

In a bowl, lightly beat the egg and add salt and pepper. Carefully dip each oyster in the eggs then lightly dredge through coconut flour. Heat oil until it begins to pop, then fry each oyster 1–2 minutes on each side until the outside is crisp and lightly browned. Serve immediately.

Dipping Sauce: Mix all ingredients together. Serve chilled.

CEVICHE

No matter what time of year it is, ceviche is the type of meal that brings on the feeling of summer. Refreshing and light, it is a "cooked" seafood dish that doesn't require turning on a stove or grill. How? The citric acid from the lemons and limes in the marinade changes the texture of protein and makes it firm, essentially cooking it.

Some versions of ceviche add tomato or other vegetables, and some play around with citrus marinades. The type of seafood you use is entirely up to you, but make sure to use ocean fish, not lake fish, which tend to turn mushy when marinated in citrus. The most sustainable and flavorful seafood choices for ceviche are Ahi tuna from the U.S. Atlantic, salmon (Coho, Sockeye or King), Yellowtail snapper, Pacific halibut, bay scallops, spot prawns or cocktail shrimp.

INGREDIENTS:

⅓ pound Pacific halibut
⅓ pound Yellowtail snapper
⅓ pound cocktail shrimp
½ cup lime juice (about 4–5 limes)
½ cup lemon juice (about 4–5 lemons)
1 avocado, finely chopped
1 red pepper, finely chopped
½ red onion, finely chopped
½ cup fresh cilantro, finely chopped

1 jalapeño, finely chopped (Remember, the seeds and inner membrane are the spiciest parts. Discard them if you don't like food too spicy.)

SERVINGS: 4

INSTRUCTIONS:

Cut the fish into ½ inch squares, removing all skin and bones. Lightly salt the fish.

Bring a few cups of lightly salted water to boil. Add peeled and cleaned shrimp for 1 minute. Put shrimp in a bowl of ice and water to chill. Cut the cooled shrimp into ½ inch pieces (it will still be fairly raw inside). Combine fish and shrimp with lime and lemon juice. Cover and refrigerate for two hours.

When you cut into a piece of the fish or shrimp, it should be "cooked" through, meaning the shrimp will be light pink and the fish will be white, not grayish or translucent. However, if you prefer more of a raw texture (as some sushi lovers do) you might want to marinate the seafood for less than two hours.

When the seafood has finished marinating, drain and discard the lime and lemon juice. Combine the seafood with the rest of the ingredients. Add salt to taste.

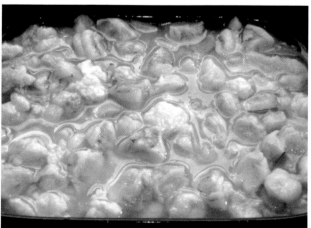

STEAMED MUSSELS

This dish can either be an appetizer or main course. Either way, it's a classic seafood dish that is easy to master. The flavor can be changed slightly by playing around with the ingredients; try fresh ginger instead of shallot, chives instead of parsley, or add tomato purée to the broth.

Increasingly, mussels sold in stores are farm raised instead of wild. Although thought to be less flavorful than wild mussels, farm-raised mussels are usually grown using environmentally friendly methods that don't expose the mussels to chemicals, antibiotics or artificial feed.

INGREDIENTS:

3 tablespoons butter

1 pound mussels, cleaned and de-bearded

1 small fennel bulb, sliced thinly
1 shallot, finely chopped
2 garlic cloves, finely chopped
¾ cup dry white wine or broth
1 tablespoon parsley, finely chopped
Dash of red pepper flakes
Salt to taste

SERVINGS: 2–4

INSTRUCTIONS:

Melt butter in a deep pot. Sauté fennel for several minutes until it begins to soften. Add shallot and garlic and sauté a few minutes more. Add liquid (wine or broth) and bring to a boil. Add mussels and put a lid on the pot, turning heat down slightly and cooking until mussels open, 3–5 minutes. Salt broth to taste.

VEGETABLES

Vegetables provide a beautiful array of colors and textures to every meal. They also provide ample nutrients, antioxidants, minerals, inflammation-fighting phytonutrients and fiber, and are low in carbs. Vegetables deserve to be the dish that you plan the rest of a meal around. They can be extremely versatile pairing nicely with a wide variety of meats. Use your own preferences and cravings as a guide.

Some vegetables you hated as a child may taste different to you as an adult. Palates change as we get older, and so do our abilities to prepare vegetables in creative ways: browned butter and hazelnuts add richness to cauliflower, puréeing kale turns it into a silky soup, and adding sea vegetables to cucumbers creates an incredible, unique tasting salad.

Whenever possible, buy vegetables according to season. As with the other recipes in this cookbook, don't be afraid to substitute the vegetable suggested for what's in season and what you have on hand. If you're able to grow your own garden or buy from a farmers' market, you'll often find the flavor of vegetables to be more intense than those found in a supermarket. As an added bonus, sellers at farmers' markets can often give you great tips about how to prepare vegetables you're less familiar with.

EGGPLANT CAPONATA

Eggplant Caponata is a wonderful blend of late summer flavor and a good use for a bountiful garden harvest of eggplant and tomatoes (or a seasonal deal at the market). Pancetta or bacon pieces aren't traditional Caponata ingredients, but add a welcome savory note to the vegetables.

If a hot oven to roast the eggplant doesn't appeal on a warm day, roast the eggplant outdoors in a covered grill instead (use indirect heat). Most Caponata recipes call for olive oil, but the high temperature needed for roasting the eggplant will destroy the delicate flavors found in expensive olive oils. We prefer using a fat or oil with a higher smoke point to avoid damaging the heat-sensitive components of extra virgin olive oil.

Be sure to make enough Caponata for leftovers, as the slightly sweet and sour flavor notes marry and improve after a day or two.

SERVINGS: 4–6

INSTRUCTIONS:

Heat oven or grill to 500°F. Warm 3 table-spoons of the fat to make it liquid. Place the eggplant on a pan in a single layer (if eggplant cubes are too crowded for a single layer, use two pans or roast in two batches to avoid steaming). Drizzle with the warmed fat and sprinkle a few tea-spoons of coarse salt on top and mix well to spread over eggplant. Roast about 20–25 minutes, turning eggplant with a strong spatula a few times for even roasting. Remove pan and set aside for later use.

While the eggplant roasts, heat remaining tablespoon of fat in a large skillet (at least 12 inch diameter). Add pancetta or bacon and bring to a sizzle over medium-low heat.

INGREDIENTS:

4 tablespoons lard, ghee, strained bacon drippings or other fat/oil with a high smoke point

1 large or two small eggplants, cut into ¾ inch cubes (peeling not necessary)

¼ cup finely chopped pancetta (Italian bacon) or 2–3 slices regular bacon, cut up into pieces (optional)

1 red or yellow onion, finely chopped

1 can finely chopped tomatoes, 14 ounces (or equivalent amount of fresh red tomatoes, seeded and diced)

1 cup green olives, pitted and sliced
3 tablespoons capers
1 cup thinly sliced celery

⅓ cup red wine vinegar (or a mixture of vinegar and dry red wine)

2 teaspoons honey

Extra virgin olive oil (or white truffle oil) for drizzling on top after cooking

Add onion and cook for about 10 minutes, lowering heat if necessary to avoid browning.

Add tomatoes, olives, and capers, bring to a simmer, reduce heat and simmer covered, about 15 minutes. Add eggplant and celery and cook another 8–10 minutes, covered.

Remove cover, raise heat, and add vinegar and honey. Cook a few more minutes until excess moisture has evaporated. Taste and add salt and pepper if desired.

Serve hot, cold, or at room temperature, drizzled with some high quality extra virgin olive oil or white truffle infused olive oil. Excellent with grilled Italian sausages, roast chicken and fish, or tossed into a salad.

CREAM OF GREENS SOUP

Community Supported Agriculture (CSA) programs are known for delivering copious amounts of greens at times. The volume of these greens can really take up space in the refrigerator, and their unfamiliarity for some people can be a bit intimidating. Here's an easy way to get through those greens pronto, and without much fuss or bother. Any type of green will work, but more leathery ones like kale and collards will need a few more minutes of cooking to become tender.

Soup is also a great first course to prepare the appetite while a roast "rests" or the main course finishes cooking.

INGREDIENTS:

2 tablespoons butter, ghee, olive oil, or high quality lard/bacon fat

1 small onion, chopped
1 large garlic, chopped

1 quart chicken broth (see recipe on page 72)

1 bunch of fresh greens, rinsed and chopped

1 cup coconut milk (or heavy cream)

Garnish: sliced scallions, chives, crumbled bacon, finely grated aged Parmigiano-Reggiano cheese, or crème fraîche

SERVINGS: 4–6

INSTRUCTIONS:

Heat butter or other fat over medium-low heat in a 2 or 3 quart saucepan. Add onions, cook slowly, until translucent. Don't let onions brown; turn down heat if necessary. Add garlic and cook a few minutes longer; again, don't let it brown.

Add broth, turn up heat to medium-high, and bring to a boil. Add the chopped greens and cook just a few minutes until wilted and tender, slightly longer for heartier greens like kale and collards. Turn off heat and move pan away from range.

Spinach Is Just The Beginning

Dark, leafy greens are considered one of the most nutrient-dense foods available. Greens can be served raw in salads, sautéed in fat or put into soups. Below are just a few to try.

Swiss Chard: Member of the beet family with long, sometimes multi-colored stems and large fan-like leaves. Mild with a slight astringency.

Kale: Member of the cabbage family with a mild flavor that can sometimes be bitter. The leaves are thicker and chewier than other greens and the tough center stalk should be removed before cooking.

Watercress: Small, delicate leaves with a very peppery flavor.

Mustard Greens: Lacy, larger leaves that have a spicy, mustard-like flavor.

Beet Greens: The leaves and stems attached to beets are mild in flavor and wilt easily.

Broccoli Rabe: A relative to cabbage and turnips that has a stronger flavor and pronounced bitterness.

[Cream of Greens Soup cont'd]

Purée the soup with an immersion blender or a regular blender (beware of hot liquid splashes). Return the soup to the pot and season to taste with sea salt and black pepper. Add coconut milk to soup and simmer over medium-low heat for a few minutes.

BRAISED CABBAGE

This popular traditional dish brings a homey feel to the table, but without the stinky lingering sulfur odor of boiled-to-death cabbage. Cabbage is a long-keeping cool weather vegetable. It is an excellent pairing with any roast or meatloaf (especially with pork) and can often be cooked simultaneously, as the oven temperatures needed are quite similar. The final step, baking uncovered with a higher temperature, can even be delayed until the roast is finished and resting out of the oven. Just remove the cabbage dish from the oven once it is tender (after about 2 hours), uncover and set aside while the roast continues to cook. Return the cabbage dish to the hot oven and complete the final step.

SERVINGS: 6

INSTRUCTIONS:

Adjust oven rack to middle position. Pre-heat oven to 325°F. Lightly grease a large (9x13 inch) baking dish.

Remove any wilted leaves from the cabbage and then cut it into 8 equally sized wedges. Place the wedges in the baking dish in a single layer. Make sure not to crowd the cabbage as it will affect braising. If there is too much cabbage, omit one or two wedges as needed.

INGREDIENTS:

1 head green cabbage (1 ½–2 pounds)

1 medium yellow onion, coarsely chopped

1 or 2 large carrots, cut into ¼ inch rounds

¼ cup chicken stock or water

¼ cup extra virgin olive oil, high quality lard, or bacon drippings (adds a smoky flavor)

pinch of crushed red pepper flakes

salt and pepper

Scatter the onion and carrot over the cabbage. Drizzle your choice of fat and stock or water over the vegetables. Season lightly with salt, pepper, and the pepper flakes.

Cover the dish with foil or a tight fitting lid, and bake in oven 1 hour. Turn the cabbage wedges with tongs after an hour. Wedges may fall apart as they are turned; work gently to keep wedges as intact as possible. If needed, add a few tablespoons of water to avoid baking dry. Replace foil or lid.

Bake 1 hour longer, or until all vegetables are very tender.

When the cabbage is fork tender, remove the foil or lid, increase the oven temperature to 400 °F, and roast uncovered for about 10–15 minutes or until the vegetables begin to brown. Serve warm or allow to cool and serve at room temperature.

BACON BROCCOLI SALAD

This slightly tart-sweet-salty salad is always popular at gatherings (except perhaps at strictly vegetarian events) even with some who profess an avowed dislike of broccoli. The most common versions of this popular recipe are loaded with too much refined white sugar and unhealthy omega-6 oils from commercial mayonnaise. This is a much less sugary version that also uses mayonnaise made with more wholesome olive oil.

INGREDIENTS:

1 cup homemade mayonnaise (see recipe on page 224)

2–3 tablespoons raw honey, Grade B pure maple syrup, or coconut/palm sugar

1–3 tablespoons unfiltered apple cider vinegar, preferably raw (may be omitted)

10 slices cooked bacon, cut or crumbled into bite-size pieces (see "Bakin' Bacon" recipe on page 46)

2 pounds of fresh broccoli (about 2–3 large crowns), rinsed well and cut into small florets about the size of a walnut or smaller (broccoli stems may be peeled and finely chopped)

1 cup nuts, chopped coarsely (try almonds or walnuts)

½ cup assorted raisins or dried fruit, or 1 cup cut up fresh fruit: grapes, cherries, blueberries, or chopped apples (optional)

SERVINGS: 4–6

INSTRUCTIONS:

Combine mayonnaise and honey or maple syrup in a large bowl and mix well (adjust sweet-tart taste with cider vinegar).

Add bacon, broccoli, nuts, and dried fruit (if using) and mix until everything is evenly distributed and coated with dressing. Flavor is best if allowed to marinate in the refrigerator or on ice in a cooler at least a few hours.

Simple Winter Squash Mash

Stephan Guyenet of WholeHealthSource.blogspot.com shared his simple preparation for winter squash.

Winter squash keeps well on a counter without refrigeration, so it's an easy vegetable to keep around for use after the spoils of summer are a distant memory. It's easy to imagine Grok, our prototypical hunter-gatherer ancestor, or his mate finding a cache of wild squashes and roasting them in the hot coals of their fire.

Winter squash can be stored for weeks on your kitchen counter or for months in a cool basement. There are countless varieties of winter squash. Some to look for are acorn, ambercup, buttercup, butternut, kabocha, spaghetti, delicata and banana.

INGREDIENTS:

1 winter squash or sugar pumpkin
2–3 fresh sage leaves, finely chopped
2 tablespoons grass-fed butter

SERVINGS: 2–4

INSTRUCTIONS:

Steam or bake the squash.

To steam, peel squash with a sturdy vegetable peeler or a paring knife. Cut in half and scoop out seeds. Cut flesh into large, even chunks and steam until easily pierced through with a fork, about 15–20 minutes.

To bake, preheat the oven to 350°F. Cut the squash in half. Remove the seeds by scooping them out with a spoon (save them if you enjoy roasted squash seeds). Place the two halves face down in a baking dish or sheet pan with a lip around the edge to catch liquids. Bake the squash until the flesh is uniformly soft, roughly one hour. While still hot, scoop the squash flesh out of the skin (if not already peeled) and coarsely mash it with the sage, butter and salt.

BRUSSELS SPROUTS WITH BROWNED BUTTER AND HAZELNUTS

Even people who claim to hate Brussels sprouts often like this recipe. That's probably because too often Brussels sprouts are boiled and overcooked, creating a strong sulfurous odor and unpleasant mushy texture. Roasting avoids these overcooking pitfalls; the aromatic browned butter and hazelnuts also bring out the nutty best in this cruciferous cousin to broccoli, cauliflower, and cabbage. Just be sure to watch the butter closely while it browns; it quickly turns from brown to burnt.

INGREDIENTS:

3 tablespoons butter, preferably unsalted

1 pound Brussels sprouts, trimmed and quartered

¼ cup chopped hazelnuts

3 tablespoons water

SERVINGS: 4

INSTRUCTIONS:

Position rack in bottom third of oven; preheat to 450°F.

Place butter on a rimmed baking pan that is large enough for the Brussels sprouts to roast in a single layer or else they will steam instead of roasting if too crowded. Roast until the butter is melted, browned and fragrant, 4 to 6 minutes.

Remove the baking sheet from the oven; toss Brussels sprouts and hazelnuts with the browned butter and sprinkle with salt and pepper.

Return to the oven and roast for 7 minutes. Remove briefly and sprinkle with water; toss, then continue roasting until the sprouts are tender and lightly browned, about 7 to 9 minutes more.

Soaking Nuts

Especially for those who have problems digesting nuts, soaking and rinsing raw nuts is a good idea. This process helps deal with the phytates and enzyme inhibitors that can cause indigestion. As an added bonus, soaking nuts can enhance their flavor. Soak raw nuts in salt water at least 8 hours. Right after they're done soaking, it's crucial to thoroughly dry them. The best ways to do this is by putting them in a warm oven (lowest possible setting—ideally not more than 120°F) or dehydrator.

[Brussel Sprouts with Browned Butter and Hazelnuts cont'd]

Serve immediately. Goes especially well with roast meat or roast fowl.

"CREAM" OF BROCCOLI SOUP

Soup is an excellent start to a meal, priming the body for digestion of heavier main course items. Puréed soups provide a great way to get vegetables and easy-absorbing bone broth minerals into kids (or adults!) while they are still hungry and before they tire of sitting at the table. Puréed soup is also a great way to use up steamed broccoli left over from the previous night's dinner. Cauliflower can be substituted for broccoli for a milder flavored creamy white soup.

This version isn't as thick as conventional Cream of Broccoli Soup, which is usually made with added wheat flour or other gums or thickening starches, but it doesn't lack in its ability to satisfy.

SERVINGS: 4–6

INSTRUCTIONS:

Heat butter or other fat over medium low heat in a 2 quart saucepan. Add onions, cook slowly, until translucent. Don't let onions brown; turn down heat if necessary. Add garlic and cook a few minutes longer, taking care not to let it brown or burn (over-browning results in a bitter flavor).

Add broth and carrot slices, turn up heat to medium-high and bring to a boil. Add half the steamed broccoli (or cauliflower) and cook just a few minutes until broccoli and carrots are 'fork tender'. Turn off heat and move pan away from range.

INGREDIENTS:

2 tablespoons butter, ghee, olive oil, or high quality lard or bacon fat

1 small onion, finely diced
1 large clove garlic, chopped

1 quart chicken broth, preferably homemade (see recipe on page 72)

1 head of broccoli (or cauliflower) or 2 crowns, cut into florets and steamed a few minutes until tender-crisp divided into 2 parts

1 carrot, sliced very thinly with vegetable peeler or julienned (cut into fine matchsticks)

1 cup coconut milk (or heavy cream/half & half)

Garnish: sliced scallions, chives, crumbled bacon, finely grated aged Parmesan cheese, or crème fraîche/sour cream

["Cream" of Broccoli Soup cont'd]

Purée the soup with an immersion blender or in small batches in a regular blender (beware of hot liquid splashes). Season to taste with sea salt and black pepper.

Return to range over medium-low heat and add reserved steamed broccoli (or cauliflower) and coconut milk, and cook a few minutes until liquid gently simmers and florets become "fork tender". Be careful not to overcook vegetables or they will develop a strong sulfurous odor.

Don't Curdle Your Cream

Heavy cream and coconut milk have a high enough fat content that prevents curdling when heated. Half & half and regular milk, however, often curdle when heated, which can ruin an entire pot of soup. If using half & half instead of full cream, avoid curdling by adding it at the very end of the cooking process and avoid bringing it to a boil.

ROASTED CAULIFLOWER WITH LEMON MUSTARD DRESSING

Roasting cauliflower is one of the best ways to prepare this versatile non-starchy cruciferous vegetable. Beware of fights over the little browned bits of cauliflower, though. This Lemon Mustard Dressing also goes well with green beans and broccoli.

Roasted cauliflower can be served alone or scattered on a bed of fresh greens like arugula.

INGREDIENTS:

1 head of cauliflower, cut into small florets

3 tablespoons oil
1 tablespoon lemon juice
1 tablespoon Dijon mustard
1/3 cup coconut milk or half & half
1/3 cup walnuts, hazelnuts or pecans
1/8 teaspoon freshly ground black pepper

SERVINGS: 4

INSTRUCTIONS:

Preheat oven to 450°F.

In a sheet pan or shallow roasting pan, toss the cauliflower with 2 tablespoons of the oil and a little salt. Roast cauliflower until tender and lightly browned, stirring once or twice for even roasting, 15–20 minutes.

Meanwhile, toast the nuts in a dry skillet for a few minutes over medium-high heat, shaking pan or stirring nuts often to avoid burning. Nuts will continue to toast a little as they cool, so remove pan from heat before they finish toasting and set aside to cool.

In a large bowl, whisk together the lemon juice, mustard, coconut milk (or half & half) and remaining 1 tablespoon of oil. Add the roasted hot cauliflower, scraping any residual oil and brown cauliflower bits into the bowl. Add the nuts and freshly ground black pepper; toss to coat. Serve warm.

CREAMED KALE

More often seen as a garnish, kale is a leafy green that is a nutritional powerhouse worth learning to like. Kale is often a regular and plentiful item in CSA subscription boxes, so it's helpful to have a number of ways to prepare it. Kale's hearty texture has more oomph than sautéed spinach's limp leaves, and none of the oxalic astringency. One way to easily win over kale-phobes is with a rich creamy sauce, seasoned with just a bit of sea salt and pepper, and perhaps a touch of nutmeg. This classic recipe is especially good with steaks, roasts, and poultry.

INGREDIENTS:

1 bunch kale, center stems removed, coarsely chopped, rinsed and drained

3–4 tablespoons unsalted butter or ghee

1 cup heavy cream
Freshly grated nutmeg *(optional)*

SERVINGS: 2–4

INSTRUCTIONS:

Melt butter in a large skillet or a saucepan over medium-low heat. Add kale and cover to slightly steam it, about 4 to 5 minutes. Check kale and stir or turn it to cook evenly, making sure kale and butter don't burn at the bottom of the pan (lower heat or add 1 tablespoon water if necessary to avoid burning).

When kale is uniformly limp and about halfway cooked, pour cream all over kale and turn up heat to medium for 1–2 minutes. When cream is bubbling, reduce heat so that it just slightly simmers uncovered. Cook for another 3 to 5 minutes, stirring once or twice to avoid sticking. Kale is done when it is tender and cream is thickened and reduced by about half. Season to taste with sea salt, black pepper, and nutmeg (if using). Serve warm.

Nutmeg

Whole nutmeg has more flavor and aromatics than pre-ground nutmeg and is sold in most spice aisles. To grate nutmeg for a recipe, use a citrus zester, also known as a microplane zester.

[Creamed Kale cont'd]

Variation: Creamed Kale and Onions
Before adding kale to pan, sauté 1 onion, minced or thinly sliced, in melted butter over low heat until soft and translucent. Add kale and continue with recipe.

Cucumber Moons with Seaweed Salad

Crisp, refreshing and mild-flavored cucumbers are the perfect vegetable to pair with the stronger ocean-like flavor of seaweed. This salad is wonderful served with fish. Try it with salmon or seared tuna.

SERVINGS: 2

INSTRUCTIONS:

If cucumber peels are thick and/or waxed, peel with a vegetable peeler (thin-skinned unwaxed cucumbers may be peeled or not, depending on preference—alternating stripes of green and white are attractive, too). Cut cucumbers lengthwise and scrape out the seeds with a spoon. Then cut cucumbers crosswise into "moons".

If using fresh seaweed, rinse well to remove excess salt used in packing (or sand if freshly collected). If using dried seaweed, soak in filtered water to re-plump and drain thoroughly. Cut with kitchen scissors into smaller pieces if too large.

INGREDIENTS:

1–2 large cucumbers

¼ cup mixed fresh or "re-plumped" dried seaweed

1 tablespoon apple cider or rice wine vinegar*

2 tablespoons toasted sesame oil
1 teaspoon wheat-free tamari
1–2 teaspoons honey *(optional)**

1–3 dashes of hot pepper sauce, to taste (or a bit of fresh hot pepper or hot red pepper flakes)

Half of the vinegar and all of the honey may be replaced with 2 tablespoons of mirin, a slightly sweet Japanese cooking wine (look for a traditionally-made mirin, without high fructose corn syrup).

[Cucumber Moons with Seaweed Salad cont'd]

Whisk together remaining ingredients. Place cucumber "moon" slices in the shallow dish with drained seaweed and dressing; toss to coat thoroughly.

The Fifth Food Group: Algae

Pound for pound, sea vegetables are the most nutrient dense food in existence. Long used in Asian cooking, sea vegetables are gaining in popularity in the West and are now commonly found in most grocery stores. There are thousands of varieties of sea vegetables growing below water but the common types you'll see in stores are:

Nori: Toasted to a thin crispy texture and black color, nori is well-known as the wrapping of sushi.

Hijiki: Small thin, black strands that rehydrate when soaked in warm water.

Kombu (also known as kelp): Dark in color and generally sold in strips or sheets with a chewy texture that softens when soaked in liquid. It can also be ground and used as a condiment. It is commonly used to flavor soup stock.

Wakame: Chewy and slippery texture and greenish color, commonly used for seaweed salad. Sold dried or fresh.

Arame: Thin and wiry, usually sold dried. Has a mild flavor that is less fishy than other sea vegetables.

Dulse: Reddish in color with a chewy texture and flat, fan-shaped frawns that are often sold ground up, to be sprinkled over food.

Laver: Black strips with a paper-like texture and fairly strong fishy, salty flavor. Can be roasted and crumbled or soaked to rehydrate.

EGGS

Breakfast is not the only meal of the day when eggs can, and should, play a starring role. Easy to cook and happy to be paired with almost any type of vegetable, herb, spice or meat, eggs are a cook's best friend. Some of these recipes, like Egg Muffins, can be cooked ahead of time and enjoyed as a grab-and-go snack throughout the week. Others, like Eggs Benedict Salad, are perfect for lunch and dinner. Poached, baked, boiled or fried, we love eggs and think you will too after trying just a few of these egg-inspired recipes.

Eggs add satiating fat and protein to every meal, plus a multitude of vitamins and minerals. To insure you're buying the most nutrient-rich eggs possible, read the carton before buying. Free-range and cage-free don't mean a whole lot when it comes to buying eggs. Look for organic and, if you can, buy from local producers at farmers' markets. Organic eggs have up to 20 times more omega-3s than mass-produced, grain-fed chicken. Plus, eggs bought locally usually have a richer just-off-the-farm flavor that can't be beat.

EGGS BENEDICT SALAD

Most people are familiar with eggs Benedict as a brunch dish, often served over the top of English muffins. We love this creative version of the classic recipe that has all the rich flavor of eggs Benedict, but is lighter and healthier. Creamy hollandaise sauce just happens to make the perfect warm dressing, drizzled over spinach and garnished with crispy bacon and soft poached eggs.

SERVINGS: 4

INSTRUCTIONS:

If using bacon, cook using your preferred method and crumble into pieces when cool. If using prosciutto, tear it into strips and sauté in a hot pan for several minutes to crisp it up. Set aside.

To poach eggs: Fill a pot or saucepan with 3–4 inches of water and add vinegar. Bring to a simmer. Break 1 egg into a coffee cup then slide egg gently into water. Repeat process with the remaining three eggs, spacing them evenly in saucepan. Keep the water at a simmer, not a full boil, until the egg whites are firm, about 2 minutes. Scoop the eggs out with a slotted spoon and transfer eggs to a plate. Blot off any excess water.

INGREDIENTS:

4 slices of bacon or prosciutto
4 eggs, plus 2 eggs yolks
1 teaspoon vinegar
3 tablespoons fresh lemon juice
½ cup (1 stick) unsalted butter, melted
1 teaspoon Dijon mustard
¼ teaspoon salt
7 ounce bag raw spinach or arugula
¼ cup finely chopped red onion

To make hollandaise dressing:
Whisk 2 raw egg yolks and lemon juice in a medium stainless steel bowl or small pot. Gradually whisk in melted butter. Set or hold the bowl directly over a saucepan of gently simmering water (but do not allow the bottom of bowl to touch the water, or the yolks will become too hot and scramble). Whisk constantly until the mixture thickens, about 6 minutes. Remove from heat. Whisk in mustard and salt.

Toss half of hollandaise sauce with the spinach to coat. Add more if you wish. Toss with red onion and crumbled bacon. Serve the salad with a poached egg on top and a drizzle of dressing.

Egg Muffins

These ingenious muffins are a favorite snack throughout the week and a perfect side dish for brunch. We've used a simple combination of ground meat, cheese and red pepper for flavoring, but switching up the ingredients a little each time you make this will keep things interesting.

Try different types of meat and sausage, skip the cheese entirely or try different types (we like pepper jack and cheddar) and use just about any chopped vegetable you like. Just be careful of vegetables that emit a lot of water, like mushrooms and spinach, as the muffins won't hold their shape as well.

INGREDIENTS:

6 eggs

¼ pound cooked ground meat or sausage

1 red pepper, finely chopped
¼ cup grated cheese *(optional)*
Salt and pepper, to taste

SERVINGS: 6

INSTRUCTIONS:

Preheat oven to 350°F.

Generously grease 6 muffin tins with butter or coconut oil, or for easier removal line with paper baking cups. The baking cups also help the muffins hold their shape.

In a bowl, beat the eggs. Add meat, red pepper, cheese and seasoning. Spoon into muffin tins. Bake 18–20 minutes or until a knife stuck into the muffin comes out clean.

Swiss Chard Frittata

A frittata is like an open-faced omelet and can be sliced into wedges that are easy to pack up for lunch. Pretty much any combination of meat and vegetables can be sautéed into a frittata, but we love the brilliant waves of green that Swiss chard adds. If you don't usually eat Swiss chard, this recipe is the perfect introduction.

INGREDIENTS:

1 tablespoon oil

2 tablespoon finely chopped onion

1 bunch of Swiss Chard, finely chopped

6 beaten eggs

A tablespoon or two of dried or fresh herbs (like oregano, basil or parsley)

Optional additions: grated cheese, diced peppers, cooked sausage

SERVINGS: 4–6

INSTRUCTIONS:

Warm oil in an ovenproof sauté pan and sauté onions until they begin to soften. Add Swiss Chard and sauté until it wilts, about five minutes. Add dried or fresh herbs. Pour in eggs, stir quickly then let cook until they just barely begin to set. The frittata can be finished three ways: turn the heat down to medium–low and put a lid on the pan so the eggs can cook through; put the pan under a broiler for 3–5 minutes; finish in the oven at around 375°F.

The size of the sauté pan you use will determine how thick the frittata is. Smaller pans make thicker frittatas that puff up more.

Egg Foo Yung

This classic dish found on many Chinese American menus is similar to a frittata, but the flavor is entirely different. We like it best for dinner, when the savory combination of mushrooms and shrimp tastes just right.

INGREDIENTS:

6 eggs, beaten
1–2 tablespoons wheat-free tamari
1–2 finely diced garlic cloves
½ teaspoon red pepper flakes
2 tablespoons toasted sesame oil
¼ cup finely chopped mushrooms
¼ cup finely diced scallions, plus more for garnish
½ pound shrimp (peeled and deveined), roughly chopped
1 cup mung bean sprouts

SERVINGS: 4

INSTRUCTIONS:

Beat eggs in a bowl with tamari, minced garlic and pepper flakes.

Heat 1 tablespoon of sesame oil to cook mushrooms and scallions on medium-low heat. Add shrimp and cook just until they begin to turn pink then add bean sprouts. Add last tablespoon of oil then pour in eggs. Stir a few times then let the eggs begin to set. The Egg Foo Yung can be finished three ways: keep the heat at medium-low heat and put a lid on the pan so the eggs can cook through; put the pan under a broiler for 3–5 minutes; finish in the oven at around 375°F.

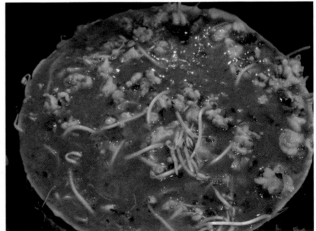

ZUCCHINI EGG BAKE

This dish is a lot like a casserole and is something that is great to serve for dinner alongside a salad. It can be made ahead of time and heated up just before eating, although it's great cold if you're too hungry to wait.

INGREDIENTS:

4 tablespoons butter

¼ cup finely chopped onion

2 pounds zucchini, grated

½ pound ground Italian sausage or other ground meat

3 eggs, beaten

⅓ cup grated Parmigiano-Reggiano cheese

SERVINGS: 4

INSTRUCTIONS:

Preheat oven to 350°F. In a sauté pan, melt butter and add onion and zucchini. Sauté until zucchini is tender, 5–7 minutes. Put zucchini in a colander to drain off any excess liquid. Add sausage to the sauté pan and sauté until just cooked. Combine the sausage and zucchini and season to taste. Add eggs, mix well, and pour into an 8x8 square pan. Grate cheese on top. Bake uncovered 35–40 minutes.

TOMATOES STUFFED WITH GROUND BISON AND EGGS

When you're tired of the standard scramble or omelet, turn to this recipe to make breakfast interesting again. We especially love this recipe during the summer when perfectly ripe, large tomatoes are easy to find. You can easily multiply this recipe and bake a whole pan of Tomatoes Stuffed with Ground Bison and Eggs for a large group.

INGREDIENTS:

2 large, round tomatoes (not Romas)
½ an onion, finely chopped
¼–⅓ pound ground bison
2 eggs
1 teaspoon oregano
Salt and pepper, to taste

SERVINGS: 2

INSTRUCTIONS:

Preheat oven to 400°F. Slice the top off the tomatoes and scoop out the seeds using either a paring knife or a spoon. Place the tomatoes in the oven, covered with foil. Bake 5–7 minutes to soften tomatoes slightly. Don't bake too long or the tomatoes will become mushy and fall apart. Take out of the oven and dump out any water in bottom of tomatoes.

While tomatoes are baking, sauté the onion in oil for a few minutes until soft. Add the bison and oregano, breaking the meat into small pieces as it cooks. Sauté five minutes, at which point the bison should only be slightly pink. Season to taste.

Turn oven to broil. Spoon meat into each tomato, pressing the meat down to fill the tomato as much as possible while still leaving about a ½ inch of space on top for the egg. Crack an egg into each tomato and put under broiler until egg is just set, about 5 minutes.

ALMOND CRUSTED POACHED EGGS

This easy recipe gives poached eggs a little more pizzazz. The yolk stays soft and runny inside, perfectly complimenting the crispy, crunchy coating. For more crunch, you could even add a tablespoon of sliced almonds to the batter.

INGREDIENTS:

1 poached egg
⅛ to ¼ cup almond flour
1 tablespoon fresh dill
¼ teaspoon salt
1 egg, beaten
Oil for frying

SERVINGS: 1 (can easily be multiplied to serve more)

INSTRUCTIONS:

To poach egg: Fill a pot or saucepan with 3–4 inches of water and add 1 teaspoon vinegar. Bring to a simmer. Break egg into a coffee cup then slide egg gently into water. Keep the water at a simmer, not a full boil, until the egg white is firm, about 2 minutes. Scoop the egg out with a slotted spoon and blot off any excess water.

Mix together the almond flour, dill and salt. Keeping the egg in a slotted spoon, sprinkle flour on top so the egg is lightly but thoroughly coated. Spoon beaten eggs over the top then sprinkle more flour on top.

Warm 1 inch of oil in a pan. Gently set the egg in the hot oil with the flour-covered side facing down. Fry 2–3 minutes, until flour is deeply browned. Scoop out with a spatula onto a paper towel to blot off excess oil if necessary. Serve immediately.

Fried Eggs Over Green Chili Burgers

Adding a fried egg to the top of a burger isn't common in the U.S., but Australians have long enjoyed this delicious and protein-packed combination. Any Aussie you ask will recommend serving the yolk slightly soft, so it runs over the burger as you eat it. Although we swiped the idea from down-under, we've given it a little wild west flavor with the addition of mild chiles and ground bison.

INGREDIENTS:

4 poblano chiles or 1 small can diced green chiles

1 pound ground bison

½ cup finely chopped cilantro

¼ cup finely chopped onion

1 teaspoon cumin

½ teaspoon chili powder

½ teaspoon salt *(optional)*

4 fried eggs

Optional garnishes: avocado and lettuce

SERVINGS: 3–4

INSTRUCTIONS:

If using poblano chiles, cut the chiles in half lengthwise and discard seeds. Place halves, skin sides up, on a foil-lined baking sheet and broil until blackened, 5–10 minutes, Place in a plastic bag; seal. Let stand 15 minutes. This will loosen the skin so it is easier to peel off. After peeling, discard skins and roughly chop the chiles.

In a bowl mix diced chiles with meat, cilantro, onion, spices and salt. Form into burgers and grill. While the burgers are grilling, fry the eggs. Serve the fried eggs on top of the burgers. If you like, garnish with avocado and lettuce.

Hard Boiled Eggs and Salmon Over Cauliflower Rice

An aromatic blend of cumin, turmeric and dill flavor, this dish, which is perfect for dinner, also happens to be just as good cold the next day for breakfast. Eggs and salmon are incredibly satisfying together, and create a one-two punch of protein and good fats that can't be beat.

INGREDIENTS:

1–1 ½ pounds salmon, skinned and de-boned

1 head of cauliflower
1 teaspoon turmeric
1 teaspoon cumin
1 onion, finely chopped
2–3 garlic cloves, finely chopped
½ cup finely chopped dill
4 hard boiled eggs, sliced

SERVINGS: 6

INSTRUCTIONS:

Preheat oven to 425°F. Put salmon in a baking pan and add 2 cups of water. Cover the pan and poach salmon in the oven until cooked through, about 15 minutes. Lightly salt to taste if desired.

While the salmon is cooking, chop the cauliflower into small florets and steam until just soft. Grate in a food processor so the texture resembles rice. Warm a little oil in a pan and add spices and onion and sauté until soft. Add garlic and sauté a few minutes more. Add grated cauliflower to the pan with the spices and onion and mix well. Flake the salmon into small chunks and mix it in along with dill and eggs.

Tamari Eggs

Hard boiled eggs are an easy snack that can be made a little more interesting with a quick roll in tamari, an Asian sauce similar to soy sauce. Eat the eggs whole or slice them into a salad. If you want to get even more creative, look for tiny quail eggs. Although it takes a little dexterity to peel the shell off the tiny eggs, they are fun to eat and serve.

INGREDIENTS:

1 hard boiled egg
1 tablespoon wheat-free tamari

SERVINGS: 1 (can easily be multiplied)

INSTRUCTIONS:

The best way to hard boil an egg is to cover it with water and bring the water to a boil. As soon as the water boils, turn off the heat, put a lid on the pot and let it sit for 10 minutes. Cool the egg in a bowl of ice water.

Carefully peel the hard boiled egg. Heat the tamari in a saucepan and bring it to a gentle boil. When it begins to foam, turn the heat to low and roll the egg around in the tamari, coating it completely. Chill and eat.

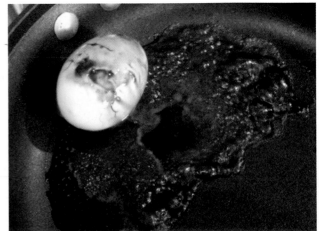

PRIMAL SUBSTITUTES

There are certain foods most of us grew up with—pancakes, mashed pota-toes, pasta—that can be hard to let go of entirely. Especially if changing to Pri-mal Blueprint eating means a drastic change in your life. Cravings are bound to strike now and again and when they do, don't torture yourself. Simply turn to this chapter, where healthier but equally delicious options abound.

Creativity and openness to trying new things is what this chapter is all about. These recipes will help you transition to Primal eating and introduce you to some new ways to prepare old favorites. Don't worry—Primal versions of your favorite comfort foods are still one hundred percent comforting. You'll find many of these recipes (like the incredible enchiladas) to be so good that you'll never miss the "original" version again.

ENCHILADAS

There is just no reason anyone should have to give up enchiladas, a delicious, one pan meal that just about everyone loves. You may find it hard to believe, but you're not even going to miss the tortillas. The egg white crepes are very easy to prepare and incredibly sturdy; they'll hold as much meat as you want to stuff in them.

SERVINGS: 6–8

INSTRUCTIONS:

Preheat oven to 375°F.

If using poblano chiles, cut chiles in half lengthwise and discard seeds. Place halves, skin sides up, on a foil-lined baking sheet and broil until blackened, 5–10 minutes. Place in a plastic bag; seal. Let stand 15 minutes. This will loosen the skin so it is easier to peel off. After peeling, discard skins and roughly chop the chiles.

Cut an "x" on the top of the tomatoes, just breaking the skin. Under a broiler roast the whole tomatoes, blackening the skin on all sides, about 20 minutes total. Cool, then peel off the skin and put the whole tomatoes in a food processor or blender with the diced chiles and purée until smooth.

INGREDIENTS:

2 poblano chiles or 1 small can diced green chiles

12 Roma tomatoes or 6 regular large tomatoes

1 onion, finely chopped

3 garlic cloves, finely chopped

2 pounds of chicken breasts and/or thighs

1 teaspoon chili powder

1 teaspoon cumin

½ teaspoon salt

8 egg whites

⅓ cup half & half or cream

½ cup grated cheddar or Monterey jack cheese

Optional garnishes: finely chopped scallions, cilantro, avocado, salsa

[Enchiladas cont'd]

Over medium heat in a deep saucepan, sauté onions and garlic in a few table-spoons of oil. Add the chicken, browning lightly each side of the breasts or thighs, about 2–3 minutes a side. Add the chili powder, cumin and salt then pour in the tomato mixture. Cover with a lid and bring to a simmer for about 20 minutes until chicken is cooked. Remove chicken from the pot and slice thinly. Salt lightly if needed. Reserve 1 cup of sauce on the side then return the sliced chicken to the pan of sauce and mix well to coat.

In a bowl, whisk together egg whites and half & half. Heat a 10 inch skillet over medium-low heat, coat lightly with oil and add just enough egg mixture to coat the pan in a very thin layer, about $1/6$ of a cup. Cook for one minute then add a lid and cook for about 25 seconds more. Use a rubber spatula to coax the egg white crepe out of the pan. This should yield around 10 crepes.

Lightly oil the bottom of a 13x9 baking pan. Set an egg white crepe on a plate and fill it with one-third cup chicken and a light sprinkle of cheese. Roll up and place in the baking pan. Continue until all the crepes are stuffed. If there is left-over chicken and cheese, spoon it around the rolled crepes. Cover the pan lightly with foil and bake 20 minutes.

MASHED PARSNIPS

Mashed Parsnips are an easy substitute that provide all the creamy comfort of mashed potatoes without as many carbs. Parsnips can be prepared in the same method as mashed potatoes and served in the exact same way. The earthy and slightly sweet flavor lends itself to savory garnishes of butter and salt, or if you're in the mood, add nutmeg and cinnamon. If parsnips aren't your thing, try using cauliflower instead.

INGREDIENTS:

2 pounds parsnips, peeled and cut into small chunks

1 cup chicken broth
Salt and butter, to taste
¼ cup cream *(optional)*

¼ teaspoon nutmeg and cinnamon *(optional)*

SERVINGS: 2–4

INSTRUCTIONS:

In a deep pan, combine parsnips with chicken broth and 1 ½ cups water. With a lid on, simmer until very tender (about 15 minutes). Drain off broth and reserve it on the side. Mash parsnips with a fork or potato masher. Add broth or cream until desired consistency is reached. Add salt and butter to taste. Top with a pat of butter and if you wish, a dusting of nutmeg and cinnamon.

CAULIFLOWER RICE

Any dish that has a bit of sauce or broth is terrific served with cauliflower rice. The recipe is so simple and so similar in taste and texture to real rice that you're going to find yourself making cauliflower rice all the time. Cauliflower rice does not soak up liquid quite as well as regular rice does when baked, so it's not as ideal for casseroles, but that's one of the only downsides to this innovative dish. We've used Cauliflower rice numerous recipes in this cookbook, including Jambalaya and Moroccan Chicken.

INGREDIENTS:

1 head of cauliflower

SERVINGS: 4–6

INSTRUCTIONS:

Cut the cauliflower into small florets. If you're adding the cauliflower rice to a dish that will simmer on the stove, there is no need to pre-cook it. If you're serving the cauliflower rice alone as a side dish, steam it briefly before grating. Run the florets through the food processor, using the grating blade. If you don't have a food processor you can use a cheese grater, but it makes the task more difficult.

That's it! If serving the cauliflower rice alone, add salt and butter to taste.

SUMMER SQUASH NOODLES

For many people, giving up pasta is the hardest eating change to make until they discover how to turn yellow squash or zucchini into noodles. Make a batch of your favorite sauce, serve it over these summer squash noodles and you'll be shocked at how similar the flavor and texture is to pasta. The recipe is easy, but for noodles with a firm texture plan to let them sit for a few hours before cooking. During the winter months, try serving your favorite pasta sauce over spaghetti squash. Cut the squash in half and bake it, then scoop out the inside and you'll find out exactly why it's called spaghetti squash.

INGREDIENTS:

1–2 summer squash (yellow or zucchini) per person

1–2 garlic cloves, finely chopped
Olive oil

SERVINGS: Multiply to serve as many as needed

INSTRUCTIONS:

Zucchini usually works better than yellow summer squash because it is less watery and has fewer seeds. If you do use yellow squash, first scrape the seeds out with a knife so the inside is smooth. You can peel the yellow squash or zucchini if you want to create the most realistic looking noodles possible. Otherwise, leave the peel on for the added color and ease of preparation.

Use the thin julienne setting on a mandoline or a sharp knife to slice the zucchini into thin strips similar to spaghetti. Next, the "noodles" need to dry out or the texture will be mushy when you sauté them. Ideally, leave them on your counter for at least 3 hours. If you want to prep the dish in the morning for dinner, wrap the noodles in paper towels and leave them in the fridge while you're at work all day.

After the noodles set and lose some of their moisture, warm olive oil and garlic in a pan and sauté the noodles just a few minutes to heat and coat with oil. That's it! Serve with any pasta sauce or sautéed vegetables.

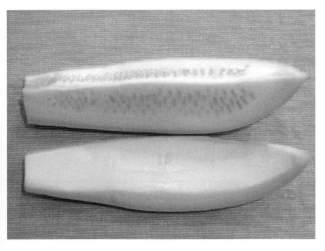

JAMBALAYA

Jambalaya is one of those great dishes that involves throwing a lot of things into a pot and letting the magic happen on its own while you eagerly wait. With this recipe you won't have to wait long before ladling the brothy, slightly spicy blend of seafood and sausage into bowls over...rice? Nope. This is where our recipe diverts from a traditional jambalaya. A warm, soft bowl of grated cauliflower mimics the texture of rice, and the flavor is so mild you'll be shocked by how much it tastes like rice, too. It pairs perfectly with this classic Creole favorite.

INGREDIENTS:

½ pound andouille pork sausage (or other spicy sausage), cut into slices

1 small onion, finely chopped

2 green bell peppers, finely chopped or cut into strips

2 garlic cloves finely chopped
1 teaspoon paprika
1 teaspoon salt
1 teaspoon dried oregano
½ teaspoon dried thyme

⅛ teaspoon cayenne pepper (or less if you don't want it too spicy)

1 (28 ounce) can diced tomatoes
1 cup chicken broth
½–1 head cauliflower
1 pound shrimp, shells and tails off
4 scallions, finely chopped

SERVINGS: 6

INSTRUCTIONS:

Cook sausage in a large, deep pot. As it browns, add a little more oil to the pan and then sauté yellow onion and bell peppers until onion becomes soft. Add garlic and spices then tomatoes and chicken broth. Bring to a simmer with the lid on for 10 minutes.

While it simmers, cut the cauliflower into small florets and grate in a food processor so the texture resembles rice. Add the cauliflower to the pot and simmer another 10 minutes. Add the shrimp and simmer until cooked through and pink, about five minutes. Garnish with scallions.

SPINACH BREAD

Bread, really, is just an edible vehicle to transport sandwich fixings (meat and vegetables) into your mouth without getting your hands messy. It's also a slice of insulin-spiking starch that you're better off skipping. Don't expect this recipe for spinach bread to taste exactly like bread made with flour and yeast. Instead, it's a moist and flavorful substitute that is certainly capable of carrying slices of meat and veggies to your mouth—it's also delicious sliced and eaten alone.

INGREDIENTS:

3–4 eggs, whisked (for a firmer version of spinach bread, add a few more eggs)

16 ounces frozen spinach
2 tablespoons butter
½ cup pine nuts
2 cloves crushed garlic
Small bunch of basil (about 15 leaves)
¼ teaspoon salt *(optional)*

SERVINGS: 6–8

INSTRUCTIONS:

Preheat oven to 350°F. Defrost spinach over low heat. Put in a colander lined with cheese cloth or a thin towel and wrap the towel around the spinach. Squeeze out as much moisture as possible.

Melt butter over low heat and add pine nuts and garlic, toasting until golden brown. Pine nuts burn easily, so keep an eye on them. Put in a food processor with the basil and pulse a few times until the nuts are broken up but not completely smooth. Add spinach and salt and pulse for ten seconds. Stir in eggs. Scrape into a buttered pie pan or 7x11 baking dish. Bake 20–30 minutes, until set. Let cool, then cut.

NUT CRACKERS

If chips are the most addictive snacks around then crackers are a close runner up. These nut crackers are rich and satisfying and loaded with protein and heart healthy fat. So snack away!

INGREDIENTS:

2 cups fine almond meal

1 teaspoon baking soda

1–2 tablespoons dried oregano or Italian seasoning

1 cup finely grated Parmesan or Romano cheese

2 tablespoons olive oil

3 tablespoons water

SERVINGS: A dozen or so crackers

INSTRUCTIONS:

Preheat oven to 350°F. In a mixing bowl, combine all ingredients and stir to form a moist, sticky dough. Add more water or oil if needed. Using wet hands, place the dough on a baking sheet lined with parchment paper. Using your fingers, flatten the dough out into a thin rectangle measuring about 10x8.

Sprinkle a little sea salt on top if desired. Bake for 15 minutes or until dough becomes dry and golden in appearance. Remove and cool on a wire baking rack. Once the dough is cooled (and this is important, because it becomes very brittle right out of the oven) use a pizza cutter to create crackers. If not consuming immediately, be sure to store in an air-tight container.

COCONUT PANCAKES

Some mornings a tall, steaming stack of pancakes is too hard to resist. Pancakes made with coconut flour are just as delicious with a pat of butter and fresh berries as pancakes made with wheat flour.

INGREDIENTS:

3 eggs

3 tablespoons melted butter or oil

¼ cup plus 2 tablespoons coconut milk

½ teaspoon honey
1 teaspoon vanilla extract
¼ teaspoon salt
½ cup coconut flour
1 teaspoon baking powder
½ cup or so water

Optional additions: flaked coconut, berries, nuts, cinnamon

SERVINGS: 5 large pancakes or 10 small

INSTRUCTIONS:

Whisk together eggs, oil, coconut milk, honey and vanilla. In a separate bowl, stir together dry ingredients then add the wet ingredients, stirring until smooth. Add the water to thin the batter out until it reaches your desired consistency. In a well-buttered pan or griddle, cook pancakes until browned on both sides (about 3 minutes a side). Smaller pancakes are easier to flip than larger ones, since the pancakes will fall apart if they are too big.

Nut Butter Bars

These days there are dozens and dozens of protein bars lining the shelves of grocery stores. Most of them do have protein so the name is not a total lie, but calling them healthy is a bit of a stretch when you see how much sugar and unpronounceable ingredients they contain.

These protein packed bars contain simple ingredients and will work as a quick breakfast, afternoon snack and even as dessert (if you add dark chocolate or dried fruit). The only downside is they need to be refrigerated to stay firm, but they're so delicious we don't think you'll mind.

INGREDIENTS:

1 cup slivered almonds
1 cup hazelnuts
1 ½ cups pecans
⅔ cup flax meal
⅔ cup shredded coconut (unsweetened)
¼ cup unsalted almond butter (or other nut butter)
½ teaspoon salt *(optional)*
1 ½ teaspoon blackstrap molasses
¼ cup melted coconut oil
Optional additions: ½ cup dark chocolate chips or dried fruit

SERVINGS: 12 bars

INSTRUCTIONS:

Place almonds, hazelnuts, pecans, flax meal, shredded coconut, nut butter, salt and molasses in a food processor. Depending on the size of your food processor, you may have to put in half of the nuts, pulse a few times, and then add the rest. Process until the consistency is fairly smooth (but not completely) then slowly drizzle in the oil until a coarse paste forms. Stir in chocolate or dried fruit, if using. Scrape the batter into an 8x8 pan lined with parchment and press down evenly to fill the pan. Chill in refrigerator for at least 1 hour and preferably more, until bars harden.

PUMPKIN NUT MUFFINS

This is a variation based on Bruce Fife's muffins from his excellent coconut flour cookbook. Unlike sugary and starchy wheat flour muffins that are mostly devoid of nutrients, just one of these wheat and gluten-free beta carotene-rich muffins has half an egg's worth of high quality protein and micronutrients, and just a hint of sweetness from a bit of pure maple syrup or honey.

These muffins are a great substitute for sugary cupcakes, especially if you add a ¾ cup of dark chocolate chips.

INGREDIENTS:

½ cup coconut flour, sifted
1 teaspoon ground cinnamon
½ teaspoon ground nutmeg
¼ teaspoon ground cloves or
2 teaspoons pumpkin pie spice mixture instead of individual spices

½ teaspoon baking soda
½ teaspoon salt
½ cup cooked puréed pumpkin
6 eggs, beaten

4 tablespoons coconut oil (or unsalted butter), gently melted

⅓ cup pure maple syrup, preferably Grade B (or less) or honey

1 teaspoon vanilla extract

¼ cup coarsely chopped pecans or walnuts (optional)

¾ cup semi-sweet or bittersweet chocolate chips

SERVINGS: 12

INSTRUCTIONS:

Preheat oven to 400°F.

Grease muffin pan(s) very well or use aluminum disposable muffin liners (muffins stick too much to paper muffin liners). Using aluminum foil muffin liners instead of paper liners also allows the muffins to sit unsupported on a sheet pan without a muffin tin. A double batch baked in aluminum liners will fit on a large sheet pan for easier and faster baking of larger quantities.

Sift coconut flour, baking soda, salt, and spices into small bowl. Stir to blend well and set aside.

Place pumpkin purée in a medium

mixing bowl. One by one, crack the eggs into the bowl, mixing well with the pumpkin purée after each egg is added. Add melted coconut oil or butter, maple syrup, and vanilla extract and mix thoroughly.

Add flour mixture to egg mixture and blend well with a whisk until most of the floury lumps have disappeared, but don't stir more than necessary to blend. Gently fold in nuts, if using.

Spoon into greased muffin pan or cup liners to two-thirds full. Bake for 18–20 minutes, until lightly golden brown on top and toothpick inserted into center of muffin is "clean" when removed.

Turn out and cool on wire rack. Serve warm or room temperature. No frosting needed.

ROOT VEGETABLE CHIPS

Crispy, salty chips are one of the most addictive snacks around. There is no reason to feel completely guilty about this indulgence when you substitute root vegetables for potatoes, creating colorful chips that are just as delicious.

SERVINGS: Varies depending on size of root vegetables, but typically makes several dozen chips

INSTRUCTIONS:

Peel and slice the root vegetables as thinly and evenly as possible. A mandoline works best for this, but carefully cutting with a knife will work too.

INGREDIENTS:

1 beet
1 rutabaga
1 turnip
Several cups home-rendered lard, palm oil, ghee, coconut oil, or olive oil for frying

In a large, wide pot heat about 1 inch of oil to 375°F (or until you toss a small piece of food into it and it sizzles immediately). Place a cooling rack over a baking sheet near the stove to set the chips after frying.

Using tongs, place 12 or so slices into the pot (don't overcrowd) and fry on one side until the edges turn brown, then flip and fry another minute or two on the other side. The beets will begin to brown (and fairly quickly burn) sooner than other root vegetables.

Pluck the chips out of the oil with tongs or a slotted spoon and set on the rack, sprinkle lightly with salt and let cool. The chips are best if eaten the same day they are made.

For a less greasy chip, slice the root vegetables and toss in a bowl with a light coating of oil and salt (toss the beets separately or they will turn everything pink). Space the chips out on a pan and preheat the oven to 250°F. Bake until crispy and dry all the way through, checking every 15–20 minutes, and turning once or twice.

MARINADES, SAUCES AND DRESSINGS

Marinades, sauces and dressings are viewed as a secret weapon in the kitchen because they can add incredible layers of flavor to simply prepared vegetables and cuts of meat. All can be made ahead and kept in the fridge, so they're handy when you need to perk up a meal. The same cut of meat or the same old salad will continually be transformed into something new depending on what type of marinade, sauce or dressing you serve it with. This is a great way to switch up flavor and keep your family and your own palate interested. As an added bonus, homemade marinades, sauces and dressings have flavor and nutrients that aren't diminished by preservatives, sugars and ingredients you can't pronounce.

Marinades are also a secret weapon for making inexpensive cuts of meat more tender and flavorful. Make sure the meat or seafood is completely immersed in the marinade; large Ziploc plastic bags work best for this. In most cases, two hours is about all you need to impart flavor and tenderize. After that, the meat is basically just hanging out in the marinade, soaking up little additional flavor and possibly moving past tender right into mushy territory.

The sauces and dressings in this chapter are extremely flavorful, which means they can be used in moderation. A drizzle over a piece of meat or plate of vegetables is all you'll need to transform your meal into something fabulous.

MUSTARD AND HERB MARINADE

Mustard and herbs are aromatic powerhouses and can be used on any type of meat, although marinades with mustard taste especially good with pork. Slather this marinade on steaks, chops or roasts, either before grilling or roasting in the oven.

INGREDIENTS:

2 tablespoons mustard (yellow or Dijon)

1 tablespoon red wine vinegar
2 tablespoon oil
1 tablespoon wheat-free tamari
2–4 garlic cloves, finely chopped

3 tablespoons fresh oregano (or 1 tablespoon dried)

1 tablespoon fresh tarragon
¼ cup roughly chopped fresh basil
4 twigs of fresh rosemary

SERVINGS: ½ cup (enough for about 1 pound of meat or seafood)

INSTRUCTIONS:

Mix together all the ingredients — leave rosemary twigs whole.

HERB AND CAPER MARINADE

This briny, tangy marinade has an incredibly brilliant flavor from the fresh herbs, parsley and mint. It resembles chimichurri sauce from Argentina and pairs well with red meat—try it with sliced skirt or flank steak. The marinade is also versatile enough for fish. Just make sure to save a little on the side to drizzle on top after the meat or seafood is cooked, as this marinade also tastes great as a sauce.

INGREDIENTS:

1 cup gently packed parsley
¼ cup gently packed mint leaves
2 teaspoons mustard, yellow or Dijon
2 anchovy fillets
1 ½ tablespoon capers, drained
1 tablespoon lemon juice
¼ cup oil
Salt and pepper, to taste

SERVINGS: ½ cup (enough for about 1 pound of meat or seafood)

INSTRUCTIONS:

Pulse all ingredients, except oil, in a food processor until finely chopped. Slowly drizzle in oil with processor running until the sauce reaches desired consistency.

SESAME GINGER MARINADE

The spicy, enticing flavor of ginger and rich, nutty flavor of sesame oil give this marinade its personality. It's suitable for any type of meat or seafood, and can be used as a base for more complex Asian-flavored marinades. Consider enhancing it with garlic, lemongrass or cilantro.

INGREDIENTS:

¼ cup unseasoned rice vinegar

¼ cup toasted sesame oil

2 tablespoons finely grated peeled fresh ginger

2 tablespoons wheat-free tamari

1 jalapeño chile, seeded and minced

SERVINGS: ½ cup (enough for about 1 pound of meat or seafood)

INSTRUCTIONS:

Whisk together all ingredients.

BLACKBERRY MARINADE

This marinade was inspired by the irresistibly sticky, sweet and savory experience of eating Korean-style ribs. Typical recipes for Korean ribs call for copious amounts of sugar, but in this marinade the sweetness comes from antioxidant-rich blackberries. The fruit both flavors and tenderizes the meat and helps create the finger-lickin' coating we all love. Try it with beef or pork, although don't feel compelled to only use ribs; different cuts of meat work well in this marinade, too.

INGREDIENTS:

1 cup blackberries, fresh or defrosted
¼ cup wheat-free tamari
¼ cup unseasoned rice vinegar
1 tablespoon toasted sesame oil
2–4 stalks of scallions, roughly chopped
2–4 garlic cloves, finely chopped

SERVINGS: 1 cup (enough for about 1–2 pounds of meat)

INSTRUCTIONS:

Blend all ingredients in the blender.

Grilled Meat Should be Done Well, Not Well Done

Some forms of charred or overcooked meat may contain heat-altered chemical by-products that may have carcinogenic effects if consumed frequently over time. Pay attention to meat as it cooks to avoid burning. Use a thermometer to gauge doneness and avoid grilling meat over high-heat for extended amounts of time.

There is also some strong evidence that marinating meat before grilling reduces the amount of carcinogens in charred meat. Researchers aren't entirely sure why—marinades may create a barrier between the meat and the heat source, draw out chemical precursors of carcinogens, or it could be that the herbs and spices in marinades have an antioxidant effect. Whatever it is, you now have one more reason (besides flavor) to marinate that steak.

PARSLEY OIL

Parsley is just one herb you can use for this richly-colored and subtly flavored oil that triples as a sauce, dressing and marinade. Basil and tarragon will also work really well. The oil can be used as a light marinade for meat, or drizzled on the meat after cooking. It can also be drizzled over vegetables and salads and used to sauté. Consider adding minced garlic or red pepper flakes for more flavor.

INGREDIENTS:

7 cups water
1 teaspoon salt
1 bunch of parsley (about 25–30 stems)
1 cup olive oil

SERVINGS: 1 cup of oil

INSTRUCTIONS:

The first step is blanching the herb to bring out the color. Fill a pot with the water and salt. Bring to a boil and add the parsley, pushing it down so it's completely under water. Boil for just 20 seconds (you'll notice the color of green intensifying) then immediately submerge the parsley in a bowl of cold water for 20 seconds. Drain and squeeze out excess water from the parsley.

Chop the parsley into smaller pieces, then put it in the blender for 2 minutes with the olive oil. The mixture will become very smooth and completely green in color.

Pour the oil through a fine mesh strainer or through cheese cloth stretched tight over the top of a bowl. All of the parsley particles should be caught by the strainer, so what drips out very slowly is pure oil flavored by parsley. This process may need to be done in small batches depending on how big the strainer is.

Basic Vinaigrette

Mastering a basic vinaigrette allows you to create dozens of differently flavored dressings, all using this recipe as a starting point. The key to making vinaigrette is balancing the oil and acidity, usually close to a 2:1 oil to vinegar ratio.

To change up this recipe, use lemon instead of vinegar; add more mustard or none at all; substitute garlic for shallot and consider adding fresh herbs.

INGREDIENTS:

¼ cup vinegar—red wine, sherry or balsamic

1 tablespoon chopped shallot
1 teaspoon mustard
½ teaspoon salt
¼ teaspoon black pepper
½–¾ cup oil

SERVINGS: 1 cup

INSTRUCTIONS:

Whisk together the first five ingredients by hand, then slowly add oil and continue whisking until blended. Purée first five ingredients in a food processor then slowly add oil in a steady stream. Tightly covered in a refrigerator, vinaigrette will keep for several weeks. Shake well before use as the oil and vinegar will separate.

CAESAR DRESSING

Caesar salad is one of the more popular salads. Unfortunately, store-bought Caesar is often a thick and goopy mess of vegetable oils. This version is a classic and pure version of Caesar dressing. What makes it different from a regular vinaigrette is the addition of anchovies, which will add rich flavor to the dressing but will not make it at all fishy. Buy the best anchovies you can find, ideally packed in salt, not oil. Although this recipe calls for mashing the anchovies into a paste, avoid just buying anchovy paste. This condiment is often overly salty and doesn't have a pure, fresh flavor.

For a thicker, richer dressing, egg yolk and/or shaved Parmigiano-Reggiano cheese can be added.

INGREDIENTS:

2 teaspoons red wine vinegar
3 tablespoons lemon juice

1 tablespoon anchovies, mashed into paste

1–2 finely chopped garlic cloves, or more to taste

⅔ cup olive oil
Salt and pepper, to taste

¼–½ cup grated Parmigiano-Reggiano cheese and/or 2 raw eggs yolks *(optional)*

SERVINGS: 1 cup

INSTRUCTIONS:

Whisk together vinegar, lemon juice, anchovies and garlic. (If using eggs and cheese, add now). Slowly drizzle in olive oil while continuing to whisk until well incorporated. Add salt and pepper to taste. Serve over romaine lettuce. Top with diced chicken or a salmon fillet.

Anchovies

Anchovies are plentiful around the Mediterranean and coastlines in southern Europe. The little fish are salt cured, which helps preserve them. Anchovies that are sold packed in salt, rather than submerged in oil, are usually more expensive and have a more delicate and less fishy flavor. Whether using salt or oil packed anchovies, rinse and pat dry before using in recipes.

AVOCADO MINT DRESSING

Cool avocado and mint lend their refreshing, soothing flavor and lovely green color to this dressing. Jalapeño adds contrasting spice—put in as little or as much as you want.

INGREDIENTS:

2 tablespoons unseasoned rice wine vinegar

1 tablespoon lime juice

½ cup oil

15–20 mint leaves

¼–½ of a jalapeño pepper, minced

¼ of an avocado

SERVINGS: ¾ cup

INSTRUCTIONS:

This dressing can be whisked by hand, but it's easier to purée the avocado in a blender. Simply blend all the ingredients and add salt to taste.

Coconut Almond Dressing

This dressing can also be used as a sauce—try serving it as a dip for shrimp cakes **(see recipe on page 118).** The tropical and refreshing flavor is all about balance. The rich almond butter and coconut milk are balanced with a squeeze of acidic lime, and the spicy red pepper flakes are balanced by the cooling flavors of cilantro and mint. When used as a salad dressing, it pairs especially well with salads that incorporate seafood as a protein.

INGREDIENTS:

2 tablespoons lime juice
2 teaspoons almond butter
¼ cup coconut milk
1 tablespoon cilantro, finely chopped
1 tablespoon mint, finely chopped
⅛ teaspoon red pepper flakes
Pinch of sea salt

SERVINGS: ½ cup

INSTRUCTIONS:

Mix lime juice and 2 teaspoons of warm water with almond butter until almond butter has a slightly runnier consistency. Whisk in the rest of the ingredients. Add additional salt, herbs or red pepper flakes to taste.

MAYONNAISE

Homemade mayonnaise from the Primal Kitchen is a great way to avoid the high omega-6 oils found in all commercially prepared mayonnaise products. Plus the fresh taste is far superior to store-bought mayonnaise. With a little practice you'll fine homemade mayonnaise to be quick and easy to make.

Mayonnaise variations are plentiful, so experiment to find your favorite version. Change the vinegar or use lemon juice for a bright citrus note. You can also substitute macadamia, hazelnut, walnut, or avocado oils for some or all of the olive oil for flavor variations. Embellishments are as easy as adding garlic, herbs or more paprika.

Because homemade mayo does use raw eggs, be sure to keep the mayonnaise well-chilled, covered tightly, and used up within about a week.

INGREDIENTS:

1 whole egg or 2 egg yolks
2–3 tablespoons cider vinegar
1 teaspoon Dijon mustard
Dash of paprika
Pinch of salt

¾ to 1 cup pure olive oil (Note that extra virgin olive oil can create a very bitter flavor when blended with an electric device. Either use refined or "light" olive oil, or blend with a whisk instead of an electric device.)

SERVINGS: 1 cup

INSTRUCTIONS:

Place egg, vinegar, paprika, and salt in the container you will whisk it in. If you're using a hand-held or "stick" immersion blender, make sure the container is tall enough to prevent splattering yet wide enough to accommodate the immersion blender. Drizzle the oil in while blending. If using a hand-held whisk, a glass or stainless steel bowl works best.

Measure 1 cup oil into separate container, ideally with a good pouring lip.

Whisk or blend the egg mixture for 10 seconds. While continuing to whisk,

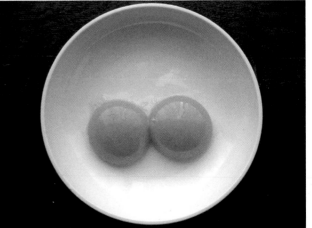

begin to slowly drizzle oil into the container in a very thin, steady stream, no thicker than pencil lead. When about half the oil is mixed in, the mayonnaise will start to thicken and take shape. Continue blending and drizzling until the oil is gone, or until no more oil will disappear into the emulsion. Season to taste with more salt, if necessary.

If the emulsion should separate, add 1 teaspoon water or vinegar and whisk again briefly.

Pasteurizing Eggs

If you are sourcing eggs from the supermarket and are worried about salmonella contamination for your homemade mayonnaise or other recipes using raw yolks, you can "pasteurize" the yolks first (you can also look for already pasteurized eggs at the supermarket).

The following process is a bit tedious, but will gently heat the yolks to reduce the chance of survival of any salmonella pathogens, yet preserve the yolk's delicate nutrients and silk texture.

Use very fresh eggs, as older eggs have more delicate yolk membranes and may break easier. Also, work gently and carefully to avoid breakage.

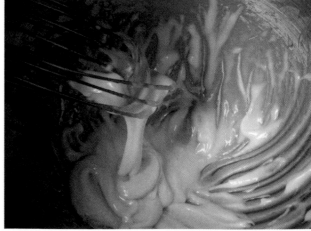

INSTRUCTIONS:

Create a double-broiler by filling one pot with several inches of water and bringing it to a simmer. Next, set a smaller pot or a bowl inside the first pot, ideally not touching the simmering water below. The indirect heat from the simmering water will heat, but not cook, the yolks.

Gently place two egg yolks in the pot or bowl on top of the simmering water with a few tablespoons of cool water. Slowly heat the water and the yolks. The pasteurization temperature range is 125–136°F so check the temperature of the water frequently with a thermometer (but don't poke the yolk!). Be precise and patient, as the yolks will cook and harden if the temperature rises too high.

When the temperature reaches 131°F, turn off the heat and move the pan from the burner. Let the yolks sit in the warm water for 5 minutes, at which point they will be pasteurized. Gently add a bit of cool water to the warm water, then scoop up the yolks in your hands, draining off excess water. Be gentle to avoid breakage or you'll have to repeat the process. Use pasteurized yolks immediately in mayonnaise or other recipes that call for raw egg.

RANCH DRESSING

Kids and adults alike love the cool, creamy flavor of Ranch Dressing on salads and for dipping, but the bottled and dry packet varieties invariably contain unhealthy vegetable oils and a myriad of ingredients that make sense only to a food lab chemist. Make your own real Ranch version in minutes and enjoy Ranch Dressing without worries.

INGREDIENTS:

1 cup homemade mayonnaise (see recipe on page 224)

1 cup cultured buttermilk, or less, depending on what consistency you want

1 tablespoon finely chopped green onions or chives

1 tablespoon minced fresh parsley
1 tablespoon finely minced onion
1 small clove garlic, minced
Dash of paprika

Dash of cayenne pepper or 1–2 drops Tabasco hot pepper sauce

1 teaspoon sea salt, or to taste

½ teaspoon freshly ground black pepper, or to taste

SERVINGS: 2 cups

INSTRUCTIONS:

In a small mixing bowl, combine all ingredients with a whisk or in a blender. Store in a tightly covered bottle or jar in the refrigerator.

CONFETTI DRESSING

Seeking new ways to use fish roe (eggs), we came up with this colorful salad dressing that features tiny red dots of crunchy tobiko (flying fish roe) that goes perfectly with bright green baby lettuce and cherry tomato salad. The dressing isn't limited to salads either; it would be very appropriate as a garnish for vegetables and fish, too.

Tobiko fish eggs are much less expensive than endangered species of caviar, and are often used lavishly in sushi. Usually tobiko is stocked at affordable prices in the fresh seafood/sushi section of Asian supermarkets. You may also find small glass jars in the gourmet cooler cases of well-stocked conventional supermarkets, but expect to pay more for a smaller container. The colorful, nutritious crunch adds a dash of flavor and flair to everyday foods and will keep for a week in the refrigerator after opening.

INGREDIENTS:

4 tablespoons homemade mayonnaise (see recipe on page 224)

2 tablespoons extra virgin olive oil
2 teaspoons cider vinegar

1 rounded teaspoon Tobiko flying fish roe (sometimes spelled Tobikko)

SERVINGS: 2–4

INSTRUCTIONS:

Stir olive oil into mayonnaise one tablespoon at a time until well blended. Repeat with vinegar, one teaspoon at a time. Taste and adjust with more olive oil or vinegar if needed. Finally, add Tobiko fish roe and stir until well blended.

LEMON CAPER SAUCE

Homemade mayonnaise is the base for this fast and easy sauce, which is delicious on fresh vegetables, fish, chicken, and salads. It's especially good as a dipping sauce for steamed artichoke leaves.

INGREDIENTS:

½ cup homemade mayonnaise (see recipe on page 224)

2–3 tablespoons fresh lemon juice
Zest from half a lemon *(optional)*

2 tablespoons capers (if using the large size, chop them up a bit)

Dijon mustard to taste

SERVINGS: 4 (2 tablespoons each)

INSTRUCTIONS:

Place mayonnaise in a small bowl. Begin adding lemon juice one tablespoon at a time, stirring to blend each time. Add mustard, lemon zest (if using), and capers, and stir to blend well.

Taste and add more lemon juice, mustard, or capers as desired. To enhance or change the flavor, consider adding fresh herbs or a few tablespoons of paprika.

Store in a tightly covered glass jar in the refrigerator and use within a week.

PRIMAL 51 KETCHUP

This homemade version of classic ketchup without any high fructose corn syrup might not fool the most die-hard Heinz 51 ketchup fanatic, but you might be surprised at how close this tastes to the original. It's even been kid-approved.

If some liquid separates after standing, just shake or stir to remix before serving, as this ketchup has no emulsifying gums like the commercial versions. Also, feel free to adjust the vinegar and spice amounts to suit your taste. The honey or maple syrup amounts may be adjusted, too, but this is a reduced sugar ketchup; take care not to over-sweeten.

Even if you don't use ketchup as a condiment very often, it only takes a few minutes to make a small jarfull if you keep these basic ingredients on hand in your pantry. Remember, ketchup is a useful base for many other homemade sauces, including shrimp cocktail sauce, BBQ sauce, steak sauce, Thousand Island dressing, and Grandma's Easy BBQ Pork (see recipe on page 39).

INGREDIENTS:

1 can (6 ounces) tomato paste
⅔ cup cider vinegar
⅓ cup water

3 tablespoons raw honey or pure maple syrup

3 tablespoons onion, minced
2 cloves garlic, minced
1 teaspoon sea salt
⅛ teaspoon ground allspice
⅛ teaspoon ground cloves
⅛ teaspoon black pepper

SERVINGS: About 1 ½ cups

INSTRUCTIONS:

Mix all ingredients in a food processor or with a hand held blender until smooth. Add a bit of water if too thick. Store in a tightly covered jar in the refrigerator.

235

HFCS-FREE BBQ SAUCE

Have you ever read a label for commercial BBQ sauce and considered the ingredients and nutrition data? It's a good bet any bottle of Kansas City-styled BBQ sauce you pick up in a supermarket (and even a "natural" food store) is heavily sweetened and uses ingredients you'd never find in a home kitchen. Yet delicious BBQ sauce is easy, fast, and downright cheap to make from scratch, not to mention you can tweak the ingredients to create your own KC Masterpiece.

INGREDIENTS:

1 cup homemade ketchup (see recipe on page 234)

3 tablespoons minced onion (or 3 teaspoons onion powder)

2 or 3 tablespoons butter

1–2 tablespoons freshly squeezed orange juice

Scant ¼ cup Grade B dark maple syrup, or to taste

1 or 2 tablespoons Worcestershire sauce or 2 teaspoons Southeast Asian fish sauce

1 tablespoon chili powder
1 tablespoon unfiltered cider vinegar
1 teaspoon freshly ground black pepper

½ teaspoon blackstrap molasses *(optional)*

¼ teaspoon sea salt (omit if using fish sauce)

SERVINGS: 10–12

INSTRUCTIONS:

Mix all ingredients together in a small pan and simmer over low heat 5–10 minutes, stirring occasionally. Store in an airtight glass in the refrigerator for up to 3 weeks.

PESTO

Creamy, rich pesto is a favorite topping for everything from fish to roasted vegetables. Basil is the most common herb used, but there is no reason you can't make cilantro or parsley pesto. Ditto for the nuts. Try pistachios, walnuts or even pumpkin seeds. If you miss the richness of cheese in pesto, try blending in a few slices of avocado to smooth out the texture.

INGREDIENTS:

½ cup pine nuts
2–3 large garlic cloves, skin removed
½–¾ cup olive oil
2–3 cups fresh basil leaves

SERVINGS: 1 cup

INSTRUCTIONS:

Place the nuts and garlic in a food processor and pulse a few times. Add the basil and pulse a few more times. With the food processor running, slowly drizzle in the oil. Stop to scrape down the sides as needed. Blend until smooth. Salt to taste.

DESSERT

For many people, dessert is an indulgence they're not willing to give up completely and that's okay. It's time we stop thinking about dessert as entirely bad and off limits, and instead think of it as a sensible indulgence. By sensible, we mean incredibly delicious options that have few downsides, like berries with a little cream, a wedge of dark chocolate, or Greek-style plain yogurt with honey and fruit. All of these will satisfy your sweet tooth and offer some health benefits. But if you're still not satisfied, read on.

The recipes in this chapter follow along the same path, but lean a little further into the indulgent category. All of these recipes, from chocolate truffles to coconut milk ice cream, are better options than store-bought desserts loaded with too much sugar, preservatives and unpronounceable ingredients. So when the sweet tooth strikes and you want to indulge without an enormous amount of guilt attached, this is the chapter to turn to, always keeping in mind that moderation is key when it comes to dessert.

APPLESAUCE

If you've sourced local apples from U-Pick orchards, roadside orchard stands, organic CSA subscription boxes, or farmers' markets, and noticed the apples go a bit soft, shrink a bit, and wrinkle quicker than apples from a store, that's because they haven't been coated with "food make-up." Apples destined to sit for months in climate-controlled warehouses before embarking on a long distance journey are coated with food grade waxes to seal in moisture and preserve their good looks. Out-of-season, shiny grocery store apples do look great thanks to modern food storage and transportation technology, but they are unlikely to contain the same level of nutrients they had when they were freshly picked.

Consider sourcing apples locally and only in-season at the peak of freshness and leave those cosmetic beauties behind. Homemade applesauce is a great way to quickly use up fresh apples that are going a bit soft or are no longer appetizing enough to eat out of hand. (Pears may be substituted for apples).

SERVINGS: Varies, depending on amount of apples

INSTRUCTIONS:

Cut apples into quarters (small apples) or eighths (larger apples) and place in an appropriate-sized saucepan—skins, cores, seeds and all. Add lemon juice, then filtered water to cover apples. Bring to a boil, then lower heat and gently simmer covered for a few hours until apples are cooked through and soft and mushy. A potato masher helps ensure that apples are not sticking to the bottom. Add a quarter to a half cup of water if apples begin to stick to pan.

INGREDIENTS:

Apples, preferably slightly tart, but any variety will work

Juice of 1 half lemon for less than a dozen apples, 1 whole lemon for more than a dozen apples

Grated cinnamon to taste *(optional)*
Maple syrup *(optional)*

Special Equipment:

Foley rotary food mill or coarse wire strainer

Allow apples to cool, then process in batches through a rotary food mill or coarse wire strainer sieve (using the back of a large spoon or ladle to press applesauce through) to strain out seeds, peels, cores, stems, etc.

Stir in cinnamon and maple syrup to taste, if using. Store in covered glass jars in the refrigerator for up to 10 days or in the freezer.

BAKED COCONUT MILK CUSTARD

Custard only takes a few minutes to prepare for the oven, and the ingredients are budget-friendly. This version is dairy-free, made with coconut milk, which is full of medium-chain fatty acids, an excellent source of quick energy. You can even make your own coconut milk for this recipe with fresh or dried unsweetened grated coconut, soaked with warm water and strained.

INGREDIENTS:

1 to 2 tablespoons unsalted butter or coconut oil to grease custard dish

5 large eggs

1 ½ cans coconut milk, not light or reduced fat

¼ cup maple syrup (can use less)

1 tablespoon vanilla extract

½ cup grated unsweetened coconut (*optional*)

Freshly grated nutmeg for "dusting"

SERVINGS: 4–8

INSTRUCTIONS:

Preheat oven to 325°F.

Put some water on to boil; it will be used to create a bain marie (water bath) for the baking dish.

Lightly grease a 1 ½ quart soufflé dish or casserole with butter or coconut oil.

In a medium bowl, whisk eggs for 1–2 minutes. Add coconut milk and mix well. Add maple syrup and vanilla and whisk to combine. Add grated coconut, if using and stir well (coconut will rise to the top).

Pour mixture into greased baking dish and set dish into baking pan in the oven. Sprinkle grated nutmeg over top of custard mixture.

Carefully pour boiled water into the baking pan (not the custard dish) until water is halfway up the side of the custard dish.

Bake the custard for about 35–40 minutes, or until set in the center (sharp knife inserted into custard center will be clean when removed). Remove from oven and cool.

Serve slightly warm or chilled. Store covered in refrigerator.

Note: Custard can also be baked in individual custard dishes or ramekins in a water bath. Baking time will be less, approximately 25–30 minutes or until middle of custard is set.

BAKED CHOCOLATE CUSTARD

When trying to cut down or eliminate baked grain foods, people often worry that there is nothing enjoyable left to eat, especially for dessert. Not true! Baked custards are richly satisfying and chock full of healthy natural fats, protein, and micronutrients. Custard even makes a delicious breakfast. Just be sure not to over-sweeten or the benefits will be offset. This is a variation on the basic baked custard, but with the rich flavor and antioxidant benefits of cocoa.

SERVINGS: 4–8

INSTRUCTIONS:

Preheat oven to 325°F.

Put some water on to boil; it will be used to create a bain marie (water bath) for the baking dish.

Grease a 1–½ quart soufflé dish or casserole with butter or coconut oil.

In a medium bowl whisk eggs for 1–2 minutes. Add coconut milk and mix well. Add maple syrup and vanilla and whisk to combine, then add cocoa "paste" and whisk well. Add grated coconut, if using and stir well (coconut will mostly float to the top).

INGREDIENTS:

Small amount of unsalted butter or coconut oil to grease custard dish

5 large eggs

1 ½ cans full fat coconut milk, not light or reduced fat

¼ to ⅓ cup maple syrup
1 tablespoon vanilla extract

3 tablespoons Dutch process cocoa, dissolved in a few tablespoons of hot water to make a smooth, runny "paste"

½ cup grated unsweetened coconut (optional)

Freshly grated nutmeg for "dusting"

Pour mixture into greased baking dish and set dish into baking pan in the oven. Sprinkle grated nutmeg over top of custard mixture.

Carefully pour water into the baking pan (not the custard dish) until water is half-way up the side of the custard dish.

Bake the custard for about 35 minutes, or until just set in the center (a sharp knife inserted in the center will be clean when removed). Remove from oven and cool.

Serve at room temperature or chilled. Store covered in refrigerator.

PEACH CLAFOUTI

Traditionally made with cherries, clafouti (claw-foo-tee) is an non-fussy way to use picked-at-the-peak-of-ripeness seasonal fruit in a not-quite-custard, not-quite-cake format. Delicious for dessert, leftovers are also welcome for breakfast. The relatively low sugar, healthy fats make this a practically guiltless dessert. Most clafouti batters only call for a small amount of wheat flour, so this is an easy conversion with gluten-free, grain-free flours. The amount of sugar in conventional recipes can often be reduced quite a bit, too. Coconut milk can also be substituted for the milk and half & half.

INGREDIENTS:

2–4 tablespoon pure maple syrup
3 cups sliced peaches
1 cup whole milk
1 cup half & half or cream
4 eggs
¼ cup flour (coconut flour, almond flour or a combination will work)

1 teaspoon vanilla

SERVINGS: 6–8

INSTRUCTIONS:

Generously butter a shallow 1 to 1 ½ quart baking dish (or pie plate). Place sliced peaches in dish. In a blender, blend the remaining ingredients for about 2 minutes (a handheld stick blender is fast and easy to clean, or a whisk will work, too). Pour the batter mixture over the peaches. Bake in a 375°F oven for about 40–45 minutes or until clafouti is golden. Let cool slightly, but it's best served when it is slightly warm.

Garnish with a shake of cinnamon, a drizzle of heavy cream, and/or whipped cream.

Coconut Milk Ice Cream

This plain ice cream base is great on its own, or add flavor with a variety of additions such as vanilla, cooled espresso, powdered green tea, crushed fruit, cocoa paste, nuts, or dark chocolate chips. Additions that are liquid, purée, and paste consistency can be incorporated when blending the base ingredients, but chunky ingredients and cut up fruit should be stirred after the ice cream machine has finished the first stage of freezing and the ice cream is "soft serve" consistency.

Unfrozen ice cream base will taste sweeter than the final frozen version, as cold temperatures reduce the sensation of sweetness. Maple syrup and honey sweeteners do add a pronounced flavor to ice cream; some object to a strong honey flavor in ice cream. Grade A Light Amber maple syrup is generally well-accepted, but Grade B Dark maple syrup really brings out the maple-y flavor and pairs well with lightly toasted nuts like pecans or walnuts.

INGREDIENTS:

2 large whole eggs or 4 yolks

½ cup (or less) maple syrup or honey

2 cans full fat coconut milk, not light or reduced fat

Special Equipment:

Ice cream maker

SERVINGS: Makes approximately 1 quart of ice cream

INSTRUCTIONS:

Whisk the eggs in a mixing bowl 1 to 2 minutes, until they are light and fluffy.

Whisk in the maple syrup (or honey) until well blended. Pour in the coconut milk and whisk again to blend well.

Freeze according to ice cream machine instructions or place in a shallow dish in the freezer for several hours, stirring once an hour until frozen firmly

A Scoop of Ice Cream

Homemade ice cream doesn't have the gums and additives that allows commercial ice cream to be firm yet still easy to scoop. So homemade ice cream may be become very difficult to scoop after many hours in a very cold freezer. Let the ice cream container sit in the refrigerator for a half hour or place it on the countertop a few minutes before serving for easier scooping. Just don't forget about it or you will later find cream soup!

[Coconut Milk Ice Cream cont'd]

(this hand stirring method doesn't require an ice cream maker but may create an icier texture). Store in a covered airtight container in the freezer for up to two weeks. Shallow, wide containers are easier to scoop from.

CHOCOLATE TRUFFLES

This recipe has been tweaked and modified over the years. The trick is combining the 72% chocolate with coconut milk and a small amount of coconut oil to get the right consistency. This version is well suited for those who prefer their truffles dark and rich, or without any dairy ingredients.

SERVINGS: Makes approximately thirty-six 1 inch truffles

INSTRUCTIONS:

Place coconut milk and coconut oil into a saucepan over medium-low heat, stirring until coconut oil is melted and mixture comes to a boil. Do not let mixture come to a rolling boil. Remove from heat.

Off the heat, add chocolate pieces to the coconut milk mixture and stir until chocolate is completely melted and there are no remaining chunks of chocolate. Continue stirring until the chocolate thickens and cools a bit. Stir in the liqueur or flavored extract, if using. Transfer to a shallow dish for faster cooling, then to the refrigerator. Let mixture thicken at least 2 hours, perhaps longer, but stir it 3 or 4 times as it cools and thickens.

INGREDIENTS:

1 can (13.5 or 14 ounces) coconut milk, full fat, not "light" or reduced fat

2 tablespoons unrefined coconut oil

1 bar (500 grams) of chocolate, 70–75% cocoa solids, broken into small pieces

Cocoa powder (Any good cocoa powder will work, Dutched or natural, but Dutched has a smoother, less bitter flavor.)

Optional additions:

Finely chopped nuts for truffle exterior instead of cocoa powder

2 tablespoons Grand Marnier or Frangelico or your favorite liqueur or brandy

¼ teaspoon pure orange extract or another flavor extract of your choice, such as vanilla, almond, hazelnut, mint, etc.

Place some sifted cocoa powder or finely chopped nuts in a shallow container. To form the truffles, remove chocolate mixture from refrigerator. If it has become too firm, let the container sit at room temperature until the chocolate reaches a clay-like consistency (do not be tempted to microwave it).

Scoop small portions of the chocolate with a teaspoon, then knock off the chocolate with another teaspoon (like when making "drop" cookies). Do not worry if truffles are not perfectly round, but do make them approximately the same size. They are meant to be reminiscent of irregular truffles from the forest, not perfectly identical like fancy bon-bons. You can also roll truffles quickly between the palms of your hands, although this is a messier technique. To finish, roll truffles in cocoa powder or chopped nuts. Chill.

The truffles are best consumed in a day or two, but will keep at least a week in the fridge (they lose a little creaminess over time due to moisture evaporation). Let them sit at room temp a few minutes before serving for best flavor/texture. For longer storage, freeze in an airtight container for up to a month. Thaw in fridge.

WALNUT MEAL BROWNIES

This rich brownie recipe will fill the air with a lovely chocolate aroma while it bakes. The brownies are a bit crumblier than their conventional counterpart, but they were kid-tested and approved, crumbs and all. If the honey flavor is too strong for your taste, try maple syrup instead.

Walnut meal is available in many grocery stores, but it's easy to make at home in a food processor (and fresher). Simply pulse walnuts until nuts are fine crumbs, but not so long that you make walnut paste!

INGREDIENTS:

1 ¾ cup walnut meal (purchased or ground in a food processor)

¾ cup Dutch process cocoa powder

1 ½ teaspoons baking powder

1 ½ teaspoons baking soda

½ teaspoon fine sea salt

2 large eggs (room temperature)

1 cup coconut milk (room temperature)

½ cup honey or maple syrup

2 teaspoon vanilla extract

⅓ cup extra virgin coconut oil (gently melted)

¼ cup chopped walnuts for topping *(optional)*

Butter for greasing pan

SERVINGS: 18 2x3 inch brownies

INSTRUCTIONS:

Adjust oven rack to middle position. Preheat oven to 350°F. Butter a 13x9x2 inch baking pan.

In a medium bowl, mix together dry ingredients until well blended. Set aside.

In a small bowl, whisk eggs for one minute, then add coconut milk, honey or maple syrup and whisk again. Add melted coconut oil and whisk until wet ingredients are completely blended.

Add wet mixture to dry ingredients and whisk well; be sure to scrape sides and bowl bottom so no pockets of dry ingredient remain. Batter will be thinner consistency than conventional brownies. Pour batter into prepared pans.

If desired, sprinkle chopped walnuts on top of batter. Bake 35 to 40 minutes. Cool completely before cutting.

GROK ROCKS

This homemade variation of boxed Polish prunes enrobed in Polish milk chocolate is very easy to make. Try serving this dessert to kids—often they don't even realize they're eating a prune. Grok Rocks are great for parties and holidays and can be made ahead if kept cool.

Prunes are fairly high in sugar all by themselves, so even with the relatively low sugar content of the chocolate, um, may we suggest you...go easy? (Hey, is that a prune pun?)

INGREDIENTS:

500 grams high quality dark chocolate, at least 60–70+% cocoa solids, broken into pieces

1 pound soft pitted prunes (now sometimes called dried plums, but they are the very same thing)

SERVINGS: Approximately 24 (assuming 2–3 per serving)

INSTRUCTIONS:

Heat 1–2" water to a gentle simmer (not boiling) in the bottom section of a double boiler or in a 2 quart saucepan. Place the top section of the double boiler over the bottom section, or fit a stainless steel or glass bowl (larger than the pan diameter) over the saucepan. Place the chocolate pieces into the top double boiler pan or the bowl. Stir every few minutes with a nonstick silicon spatula until completely melted. Be sure not to allow any water to mix with the chocolate or it will "seize" and become grainy.

While chocolate is melting, prepare rack and sheet pan. Line a sheet pan with aluminum foil (or use a silicone baking liner in the pan). Place flat cooling rack into pan.

Remove pan/bowl of melted chocolate from heat and let sit a few minutes to cool and thicken slightly. Stir in pitted prunes until they are entirely coated with chocolate.

Using a dinner fork, scoop out prunes one at a time, letting excess chocolate drip back into the pan of melted chocolate, then place chocolate covered prunes on the cooling rack. Continue until all prunes are on the cooling rack and not touching each other.

Place rack in a cool location (or refrigerator) until chocolate is solid again. Remove "rocks" from rack with the tip of a blunt butter knife to avoid creating fingerprints in the chocolate. Store in an airtight container in a cool place or in the refrigerator.

Note: This melting method "un-tempers" the chocolate. When it re-solidifies, it will melt very easily if handled with warm fingers. Tempering chocolate is a complicated process that results in chocolate that is more resistant to melting. So these simply made "rocks" will melt on your fingers if you hold them for more than a moment. Consider the ease in chocolate preparation just another benefit to these "finger-lickin' good" treats.

Coconut Milk Yogurt

This is a non-dairy yogurt version, which can even be made with a non-dairy bacterial culture, if desired (order GI ProStart Yogurt Culture Starter from GI ProHealth).

Unlike dairy milk, coconut milk does not contain lactose (a milk sugar), so a small amount of honey or other sugar needs to be added to feed the bacteria culture. Most or all of the sugar will be consumed by the live cultures.

Yogurt culturing is a very simple process and has a very long tradition—just mix milk with a live probiotic bacteria culture mixture and leave it undisturbed for several hours at a temperature ranging from 105–115°F. This constant gentle warmth can be achieved by wrapping the container in an insulating cloth then placing in a small cooler; a thermos; an oven warmed by a 60 watt oven light bulb or "dough proofing" setting; or in an inexpensive thermostatically controlled yogurt maker.

SERVINGS: About 3 cups

INSTRUCTIONS:

Gently bring the coconut milk to 125°F in a non-reactive pan over low heat, then remove from heat. Do not "cook".

INGREDIENTS:

2 14-ounce cans coconut milk

¼ cup good quality commercial plain yogurt or previous homemade batch, or commercial yogurt bacteria culture

1 tablespoon honey, maple syrup

Cover and cool milk to about 110°F. Temperature must be dropped to a temperature that will not kill the live bacterial culture that will be introduced. Cooling can be sped up by placing the pan in a larger container or sink filled with ice water. Remove about one-half cup of the slightly warm coconut milk to a small dish and mix with the plain yogurt or yogurt culture.

Return milk and culture mixture to the coconut milk, then add honey or maple syrup and stir thoroughly.

Pour the mixture into any appropriately sized glass, ceramic, or stainless steel container or yogurt maker, cover, and keep undisturbed at 105–115°F up to a maximum of 24 hours. Keep in mind, too high a temperature will kill the bacterial culture; too low of a temperature will prevent the activation of bacterial enzymes.

When culturing is complete, store in covered container in the refrigerator. Coconut yogurt has a thinner consistency than dairy milk yogurt; it's great for drinking like kefir or making smoothies. If yogurt separates, stir to remix. For thicker yogurt, strain yogurt through a paper coffee filter or a clean flour sack fabric towel. Save the liquid strained off to use in smoothies or cool beverages to add enzymes, probiotic bacteria, and vitamins.

BEVERAGES

Most of the fluid our body needs comes from the foods we eat, but sometimes, a tall, refreshing beverage is exactly what your body craves. Water is always a great choice, but it can get a little boring, especially if you're trying to break an addiction to soda or fruit juice. When you want something more, turn to this chapter before you turn to drinks filled with sugar and caffeine.

Herbs, fruits and spices add loads of flavor to drinks and can have both an invigorating and calming effect. From lemongrass to mint and juicy, antioxidant-rich berries, the beverages in this chapter offer an array of flavors without adding unnecessary sugar.

LEMONGRASS TEA

A favorite herbal tea with a unique and exotic flavor that can be served warm or cold.

INGREDIENTS:

2–3 stalks of lemongrass
4 cups of water
Fresh mint leaves *(optional)*

SERVINGS: 2–4

INSTRUCTIONS:

Trim off lower bulb of lemongrass stalks, peel the first few layers, then cut and smash the stalks with the side of knife blade, or simply use your hands to twist and snap them open to release the "juices."

Bring the stalks to a boil in water and cover. Remove from heat and let it steep for twenty minutes. At this point, you can add a touch of real sugar or honey for some sweetness, but you can leave it out. We prefer this stuff chilled, but you can drink it hot. *Optional:* add fresh mint leaves.

Lemongrass

This long, woody herb is responsible for the intriguing but often hard to identify flavor in many Thai and Vietnamese dishes, especially curries. The aroma and flavor resemble lemon, but the flavor is more exotic and complex. Look for firm stalks at a specialty grocery store or Asian market. Lemongrass is usually sold in bundles of 2–4 stalks and is inexpensive. Due to the tough texture, lemongrass stalks are typically used to flavor dishes or drinks, but not eaten. Lemongrass is also thought to help relieve cold symptoms, so when you're feeling under the weather, drink up!

REFRIGERATOR TEA

Remember easy-peasy Sun Tea Iced Tea? You put the tea bags in a jar of tap water and set it in the hot afternoon sun to "brew" into iced tea? Guess what— brewing tea in the warm sun can breed an illness-causing bacteria, Alcaligenes viscolactis. Try this cooler technique instead—the refrigerator temperature inhibits mold and bacteria growth and it's just as easy as making Sun Tea. Try two or three tea varieties together, such as black tea, green tea, and mint tea, for a refreshing twist. Consider including a floral note, such as one teaspoon of organic lavender buds with green and mint teas.

While the tea needs to soak for at least 6 hours or overnight to be fully flavored (time depends on the tea variety and amount of water to tea ratio), the chilled tea doesn't become too tannic or strong like hot brewed tea can if the tea leaves are steeped too long.

On average, about 4 tea bags will make 1 to 1.5 liters of tea, but different tea blends will brew stronger than other (hibiscus flower tea seems to brew faster, for instance). Experiment with tea amounts and varieties to find your favorite version.

INGREDIENTS:

4 or more tea bags, any variety (Black, Green, White, herbal or blends, regular or decaffeinated) or 4 teaspoons of loose tea leaves

Filtered water

SERVINGS: 3–4 per quart/liter of water

INSTRUCTIONS:

If using tea bags, just clip the tags together to the lip of the container and fill with cool or room temperature water. Steep in refrigerator or on counter (do not do this in hot weather or tea may mold). Remove tea bags when tea is desired strength. After brewing, store tea in the refrigerator.

SAGE WATER

A favorite farm-to-table restaurant, *The Linkery* in the North Park neighborhood of San Diego, serves this simply flavored water complimentary to all tables. The wait person was happy to share the embarrassingly simple recipe, but we think you'll agree the presentation is attractive and the taste is extremely refreshing.

INGREDIENTS:

Several fresh sage leaves or sprigs of leaves, as attractive as possible (un-bruised, not torn, etc.)

Cool water

SERVINGS: Can be made in any quantity

INSTRUCTIONS:

In a clear glass pitcher or water bottle, steep sage leaves for several hours. It's that simple! Leaves will stay fresh for several days, so refill the refrigerated container with water as needed to keep a continual supply of Sage Water ready for sipping.

SPICED LASSI

Lassi is a popular yogurt drink in India that is both protein-rich and surprisingly refreshing on a hot day. Pungent spices like cumin can cause the body to sweat and cool down, and mint has got to be one of the coolest herbs out there. Think of a lassi as a healthy milkshake. If a savory lassi doesn't appeal to you, use fruit and fresh mint instead.

INGREDIENTS:

1 teaspoon powdered cumin or cumin seeds

2 cups plain Greek yogurt
½ cup loosely packed mint leaves
½ teaspoon salt
¼ cup water

SERVINGS: 3 drinks

INSTRUCTIONS:

If you're using cumin seeds, toast them for a few minutes in a hot pan. Mix everything together in a blender until frothy. Refrigerate or serve over ice.

HOT COCOA

Rich, creamy hot cocoa fits into a Primal Lifestyle? Yes, though admittedly, this version might take some getting used to as we recommend you try it without sugar or only slightly sweetened. Transition to unsweetened hot cocoa by initially making it with just a teaspoon of sugar or maple syrup, then slowly reduce the level of sweetness until you can "take it straight". Using ample heavy cream or coconut milk ensures that the hot cocoa is not too watery, so add more if you wish. If you drink unsweetened coffee or tea, or have reduced other sugar sources in your diet, go right to the unsweetened version, as your sweet taste receptors are not constantly bombarded with sweetness. Using coconut milk or cream instead of heavy cream will also lend a hint of sweetness to the hot cocoa.

Be sure to use Dutch process cocoa powder and not "natural" cocoa powder, which is more acidic and bitter. Natural cocoa powder also doesn't dissolve well in liquid. Dutch process cocoa has been neutralized to mellow the acidic sharpness, creating a cocoa that tastes smooth and rich. Dutch process will always be noted on the label.

INGREDIENTS:

1 rounded teaspoon Dutch process cocoa powder

2–4 tablespoons heavy cream or full fat coconut milk

Hot water, not quite boiling

1 teaspoon or less sugar or maple syrup *(optional)*

SERVINGS: 1 drink

INSTRUCTIONS:

Place cocoa powder in a mug and break up any firm lumps with the back of a spoon. Add the cream or coconut milk to the cocoa powder and stir to create a paste or slurry. Pour in a few tablespoons of hot water and stir to blend. Add more hot water to fill mug and stir well. If sweetening the hot cocoa, sweetener may be added at any time.

If cocoa doesn't dissolve well, try again adding 2 tablespoons of hot water to cocoa and stirring first, before adding the cream and the rest of the water.

BLACKBERRY GINGER MOCKTAIL

Sweet blackberries get a little kick from spicy ginger and a refreshing jolt from lime in this amazing mocktail. (Go ahead, turn it into a cocktail. We won't tell.) Flavor is extracted and concentrated by muddling the ingredients, a bartending technique that involves pounding and crushing herbs and/or fruit with a muddler. If you don't have a muddler, just use the handle of a wooden spoon; it works just as well.

INGREDIENTS:

1 tablespoon minced ginger root
1–2 tablespoons lime juice
½ cup blackberries
Sparkling water

SERVINGS: 1 drink

INSTRUCTIONS:

In a cocktail shaker, muddle ginger, lime juice and blackberries until black-berries are completely broken up. This can be done by pounding the berries and ginger with a muddler or the handle of a wooden spoon. Add a handful of ice and shake. Strain into a cocktail glass. Top with sparkling water.

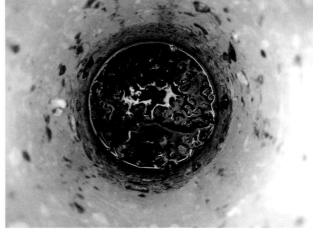